4O DAYS & 4O WAYS

Daily Meditations
For Lent *Year B*

Henry Wansbrough

*All booklets are published thanks
to the generosity of the supporters
of the Catholic Truth Society*

CATHOLIC TRUTH SOCIETY

PUBLISHERS TO THE HOLY SEE

Contents

Picture credits: Page 4: The Burial and Resurrection of Jesus scene from gothic carved altar in Church of the Teutonic Order, 1520. © Renata Sedmakova / Shutterstock.com.

All rights reserved. First published 2018 by The Incorporated Catholic Truth Society, 40-46 Harleyford Road London SE11 5AY. Tel: 020 7640 0042 Fax: 020 7640 0046. © 2018 The Incorporated Catholic Truth Society.

ISBN 978 1 78469 552 1

Introduction

During the season of Lent the Church brings before us a specially chosen series of readings of Scripture. I have long intended to write down a continuous series of reflections on these readings, but never got round to it until the Catholic Truth Society asked me to do so. It seems that the reflections written for Lent of 2017 were helpful, and it has been rewarding to reflect afresh on these texts for Lent 2018. I hope the result may be inspiring as a focus for prayer and meditation during this blessed season of Lent. For each day I have added a possible suggestion for sanctifying the day in action.

I would suggest that the best way to use this book is to set aside some time each day during Lent. Start by reading in the Missal or Bible the two passages proposed by the Church for the Eucharist of the day. The Gospel reading is probably the more important, but the Old Testament reading will illustrate it and give it a background. Remember the old mediaeval saying, *Novum Testamentum in vetere latet, vetus in novo patet*, "The New Testament lies hidden in the Old, the Old lies open in the New"! Then read the reflections and finally re-read the scriptural passages, slowly and prayerfully. This should provide a fruitful basis for Lent.

Ash Wednesday

*In other words, God in Christ was reconciling
the world to himself, not holding men's faults against
them, and he has entrusted to us the news that they
are reconciled. So we are ambassadors for Christ;
it is as though God were appealing through us, and
the appeal that we make in Christ's name is: be
reconciled to God.* (2 Co 5:19-20)

Readings: *Jl* 2:12-18; 2 *Co* 5:20-6:2; *Mt* 6:1-6, 16-18

✠

In reading Paul's letters we are always listening to one
side of a conversation, just as though we were listening
to someone making a call on a mobile phone in a waiting-
room. To make real sense of it we need to hear the other half
of the conversation. If we listen long enough and carefully
enough we can probably piece together the situation
which is being discussed. From Paul's letters we can piece
together a lot of hints about the community at Corinth
to which Paul is writing. They were an argumentative
community, made up of several different groups. Corinth
was an international port and trading post on much the best
route from the Far East, with its silks and spices, to Rome,
the capital of the Empire and importer of vast quantities of
merchandise. A century earlier the city had been destroyed

by Julius Caesar as a punishment for rebellion, but the Roman Empire simply could not manage without it, and after some decades it had to be re-founded. So there were people of all nationalities, heirs to the great temples of classical Greece, sailors, rich merchants, stevedores, and no doubt a lot of unemployed hangers-on, hoping to scrape together enough to live on. There were plenty of varied skills in the community, and in 1 Corinthians Paul devotes his full persuasive powers to encouraging the members to use their skills of administration, teaching, healing and counselling, and above all proclaiming the Good News of Jesus, for the sake of the community as a whole.

Against this background the constant ground-swell about reconciliation makes a lot of sense. There were different points of view, different interest-groups which needed to understand one another. One particular abuse was the supposedly shared community meal for the Eucharist. The rich arrived early with hampers of food and drink and took the best places, while the poorer workers had to be content with scraps to eat and places on the edge of the crowd. "You can't call this a common meal commemorating the death and resurrection of Jesus Christ," says Paul (*1 Co* 11:18-27). A keynote was that everyone must use his or her particular gifts for the whole community, not for his or her private concerns or private self-aggrandisement, but as an expression of love inspired by the Holy Spirit who gave these gifts.

In today's passage the particular emphasis is on reconciliation: God reconciled us to himself in Christ, and so we must be reconciled to God. Just before today's passage Paul says, "Everything is from God, who reconciled us to himself through Christ, and gave us the ministry of reconciliation, because God was in Christ, reconciling the world to himself, not reckoning their sins to them, and entrusting to us the message of reconciliation" (*2 Co* 6:18-19). A special way to start Lent would be to think through our relationships with other people: is there anyone with whom I need to be reconciled? Is there any enmity or grudge or offence, reasonable or unreasonable, which I could set about healing during these forty days, so that the love and peace of Christ may flow more easily?

Action:

Plan three things for Lent: one a daily practice of prayer, another giving up a luxury, a third taking up a good work.

Thursday after Ash Wednesday

> *Then to all he said, "If anyone wants to be a follower*
> *of mine, let him renounce himself and take up his*
> *cross every day and follow me. For anyone who wants*
> *to save his life will lose it; but anyone who loses his life*
> *for my sake, that man will save it." (Lk 9:23-24)*

Readings: *Dt 30:15-20; Lk 9:22-25*

✠

The second day of Lent gives us one of the dominant features of Lent, the expectation of the death and Resurrection of Jesus. The primary focus of Lent is not grim mortification, still less self-torture; it is the joyful preparation for Easter, but with the proviso that Resurrection must be preceded by Passion and death. Three times, and this is a favourite way in which Mark stresses a point, Jesus prophesies, with ever-increasing detail, that he must suffer and die before he enters into glory.

A dominant feature of each of these prophecies is the failure of the disciples. Each time they are blind to the significance of the message. The first time Peter blunders in – at least in Mark 8:32-33 and the corresponding passage in Matthew – and tries to rebuke Jesus for this prophecy, only to be told by Jesus that he, Peter, is a Satan, a tempter. Luke leaves out this criticism of Peter and jumps straight from the prophecy to Jesus' instruction that the disciples must also take up their cross and follow Jesus. On the second occasion (*Mk* 9:32-6 and the corresponding passage in Luke) we are told that they failed to understand and were afraid to ask. To make matters worse, the disciples seem to take no notice, for they immediately start quarrelling about who will get the best seats in heaven, and Jesus reiterates that they have got it wrong, and that for his disciples dignity consists in service: "whoever does not receive the Kingdom of God as a child will not enter into it". On the third occasion they again take no notice of the prophecy (*Mk* 10:32-4), and the sons of Zebedee ask to sit at the right and left hand of Jesus in the Kingdom. Matthew spares the two apostles by attributing the request to their mother rather than leaving it in the mouths of James and John.

Then when it comes to the point of the arrest they rush away helter-skelter, one of them naked, leaving his only covering in the hands of the arresting-party. Nor is this the end, for Peter, having attested that he would rather die than desert Jesus, three times denies him with increasing vehemence. So much for the men. The women are a little better, and do at least stay to watch the crucifixion at a distance (*Mk* 15:40). Their failure is to deliver the message of the Resurrection, given them by the dazzling young man at the empty tomb.

How should we explain this repeated failure, and the stress laid upon it by the evangelist? There must be a purpose in the way it is underlined. Was it to provide a lifeline for Christians of Mark's own time, some decades after the Resurrection, who had failed under persecution? Or is the message for us today, feebly trying to evade the difficulties of following Christ? It is one thing to profess loyalty to the crucified Christ, but quite another thing when we have to shoulder the one cross we wanted to avoid.

Action:

Resolve to stick to the little discomforts you have taken on for Lent.

Friday after Ash Wednesday

Jesus replied, "Surely the bridegroom's attendants would never think of mourning as long as the bridegroom is still with them? But the time will come for the bridegroom to be taken away from them, and then they will fast." (Mt 9:15)

Readings: *Is* 58:1-9; *Mt* 9:14-15

✠

The image of God as the bridegroom that Jesus here uses is a splendid one, traditional in Israel, conjuring up thoughts of joy and happy completion. This makes the implication that the bridegroom is to be taken away, presumably by force, all the more dire and disturbing.

The image comes first in the Bible from the prophet Hosea, who likens the stormy and unstable relationship of his wife and himself to the stormy relationship between Israel and God. There was a honeymoon period of forty years in the desert when Israel and the Lord were bonding together, though that too was all too often darkened by Israel's murmuring and complaining. But after that there had been a continual series of infidelities on Israel's part, interspersed with returns to fidelity. Hosea looks forward to a time when the bond will be made perfect in enduring love. In the period of the Exile the prophet Ezekiel (16:1-63) dwells on the darker side of the relationship, describing in violent and explicit language Israel's repeated infidelities with other partners and the rigorous punishment this is to receive. Also in the period of the Exile the prophet Isaiah promises that the Lord will call back his forsaken wife:

> I did forsake you for a brief moment
> But with great love will I take you back.
> With everlasting love I have taken pity on you.
>
> (*Is* 54:6-8)

With the return from Exile a new note of hope appears, most fully expressed in the imagery of the joyful wedding of a young couple:

> No more will you be known as "Forsaken"
> or your land be termed "Desolate";
> but you will be called "My Delight is in her"
> and your land the "The Espoused";
> for the Lord will take delight in you
> and your land shall be espoused.
> Like a young man marrying a virgin,
> your rebuilder shall wed you,
> and as the bridegroom rejoices in his bride,
> so will your God rejoice in you. (*Is* 62:4-5)

Against this background comes the rich symbolic meaning of Jesus' presence at the marriage feast of Cana. He inaugurates his ministry by changing the water of the Jewish purification rite into the wine of the wedding feast. The same imagery appears again in the parables, especially Matthew's two parables of the great wedding feast of the king's son (22:1-14) and the wedding attendants (25:1-13 – not "bridesmaids", for they wait on the groom, not the bride). The imagery is summed up at its most joyful in the final chapters of the New Testament, in the picture of the holy city of Jerusalem coming down from heaven "as beautiful as a bride all dressed for her husband" (*Rv* 21:2).

By his saying about fasting, then, at such an early stage of the Gospel, Jesus brings into their consciousness the final goal of his coming, the wedding feast of the Lamb. It underlines that Lent is the preparation for the joy of the final Easter, while at the same time reminding us that it is to be achieved only by suffering.

Action:

Bring the joy of the wedding feast
to all those around you.

Saturday after Ash Wednesday

*The Pharisees and their scribes complained to his
disciples and said, "Why do you eat and drink with tax
collectors and sinners?" Jesus said to them in reply,
"It is not those who are well who need the doctor,
but the sick." (Lk 5:30-31)*

Readings: Is 58:9-14; Lk 5:27-32

✠

In Lent our objective is surely to live as faithfully as
possible the standards of the Kingship of God. At the
time of Jesus there were various conceptions of what this
meant. Obviously it was not a 'kingdom' in the sense of a
territorial entity. This leads on too easily to the conception
of a physical kingdom "way up there in the skies". It is
more an abstract idea, the fact of God being king. It was
declared first of all by John the Baptist with his summons to
all who crossed the Jordan at the ford on the way to the east.
He did not cry out that they must do penance in the form of
practices such as fasting and flogging. He meant that they
must change their ways, accept new standards of life and
morality, which would mean that God was really their king.

Different Jewish groups had different ideas of what
was necessary for the Kingship of God to be realised.

Many thought that the expulsion of the Romans was a pre-condition; God must rule his people directly if he was to be really king, especially as the Romans were unclean and defiled in every way. Some thirty years after the Resurrection the diehards of this party led an armed rebellion, which was crushed in the Siege of Jerusalem in AD 70. Another group, the Essenes, went out into the desert and formed a sort of monastic community on the shore of the Dead Sea, with a strict rule, waiting to greet the Messiah. A third group, the Pharisees, probably the largest Jewish group, thought that the Kingship of God would be complete if and when everyone obeyed the Law to the letter; hence they were extremely strict about every detail.

Jesus had some contact with the Essenes. Some of their language (e.g. "sons of light" and "sons of darkness") appears in the Gospels. Exactly the same procedure for resolving disputes is found in the Essene Dead Sea Scrolls and in Matthew 18:15-17. Some scholars have argued that John the Baptist, who also came in from the desert, was once a member of their community and split off from it. In many ways Jesus was nearest to the Pharisees, for he uses the same methods of arguing from the scriptures. He certainly engaged closely with them, though this may be because of the strength of their opposition to him.

However, in two ways Jesus differed markedly from the Pharisees:

1. He did not simply condemn or write off those who were considered unclean for not obeying the Law. On the contrary, he went out to gather them in: "It is not the healthy who need the physician, but the sick."

2. He thought love and care for the neighbour was more important than strict obedience to the Law. The command to love the neighbour is on the same level as the command to love God.

These were two elements in the new standards needed for the Kingship of God.

Action:

Is there anyone I write off or despise?
Start healing this.

First Sunday of Lent

> *"I establish my Covenant with you: no thing of flesh
> shall be swept away again by the waters of the flood.
> There shall be no flood to destroy the earth again."
> God said, "Here is the sign of the Covenant I make
> between myself and you and every living creature
> with you for all generations: I set my bow in the clouds
> and it shall be a sign of the Covenant between me
> and the earth." (Gn 9:11-13)*

Readings: *Gn 9:8-15; 1 P 3:18-22; Mk 1:12-15*

During most of the year the first reading on Sundays is
chosen from the Old Testament to pair with or introduce
the Gospel reading, and it is the Gospel reading that
dominates. In Lent, however, the Old Testament reading
comes into its own. In each year of the three-year cycle
the first readings of Lenten Sundays work through the
history of revelation stage by stage. On the first Sunday of
Lent the reading is always from the pre-history of Israel,
the period before Abraham. The first eleven chapters of
Genesis, which include the story of the Flood, consist of

a series of inspired myths. They are not historical, but give a reason for some feature of the world. The Adam-and-Eve story explains why snakes have no legs, why childbearing is painful. But over and above that there is always an important moral lesson. We know only too well that we human beings do not live up to our ideals, and fail to live according to the God-given order of the universe; this is portrayed in the story of the Fall. Today's story explains why the rainbow is always a sign of hope, shimmering in the sky as a sign that murky weather is past and the sun is breaking through. More important, it is a symbol of deeper hope. The world can become so evil that God has no alternative to sweeping away that evil in a worldwide flood (a symbol of cleansing in many cultures); but there still remains a sure hope of forgiveness and divine support. As humans and animals come trooping out into the fresh air, God offers a covenant, never again to destroy the earth and its civilisation. We are also already looking forward to Easter, for then, at the Last Supper, the final and perfect covenant will be made.

Also on this first Sunday of Lent there is always the Gospel of Jesus' temptations in the desert. It might perhaps better be called "the Testing of Jesus in the Desert", for the forty days of Jesus' preparation are obviously modelled on the forty years of Israel's preparation in the desert of Sinai. The desert is a wonderful and daunting place to be alone with God. The scenery is stark. There is no refuge, no escape, no hiding, no distraction except thirst and fear. The expanses of nothingness on the arid ground below and in the empty sky above compel a realisation of human inadequacy and fallibility. Israel, God's son, was tested and failed; Jesus, God's only-begotten son, was tested and reached his vocation.

What does it mean that Jesus was with the wild beasts, and that the angels tended him? It is a return to the peace of Paradise when there was no enmity between human and animal. Far from the angel barring the gate against Adam and Eve with a fiery sword, here the angels tend the Son of God. It is a brief proleptic glimpse of the renewal of the world in the Kingship of God.

Action:

Give some of your Sunday leisure time to bringing the Kingship of God into reality.

Monday

> *When the Son of Man comes in his glory, escorted by*
> *all the angels, then he will take his seat on his throne*
> *of glory. All the nations will be assembled before him*
> *and he will separate men one from another as the*
> *shepherd separates sheep from goats.* (Mt 25:31-32)

Readings: *Lv* 19:1-2, 11-18; *Mt* 25:31-46

✠

According to Matthew's viewpoint we are awaiting the end of time, the coming of the final judge. In Mark's Gospel the coming of Christ already introduces the endpoint of time; it is the beginning of the crisis: the Kingship of God has drawn near. By the time Matthew comes to write there is the same urgency, but there is a longer time lapse before the end, to give us a chance to live out our Christian values. The parable of the sheep and goats gives us a view of that final judgement, but to see its full significance we need to look at another passage of the Gospel.

One of the stories in the final confrontation between Jesus and the Jewish authorities in Mark 12 gives us the challenge issued to Jesus by a lawyer, a question often asked: of the 613 commandments of the Law, which is the most important? Jesus answers impeccably with the confession of faith proclaimed daily by every faithful Jew, "The Lord our God is the one Lord. You shall love the Lord your God with all your heart, with all your soul, with all your strength" (*Dt* 6:4-5). This is entirely correct and gives what might be taken as the first and greatest commandment. But then Jesus adds "You shall love your neighbour as yourself" (*Lv* 19:18 – in our first reading today). As so often, Jesus goes beyond what was asked and expected. He bursts the comfort zone, just as he did with "Give to Caesar what is Caesar's, *and to God what is God's*" (*Mk* 12:17). They had not asked that!

What right had Jesus to add this text of Leviticus to Deuteronomy? It was a principle of Jewish explanation of the scriptures, certified by the great Rabbi Hillel a few years earlier, that, if there is verbal similarity between two texts, they should be interpreted together in the light of one another. These are the only two occasions in the whole of the Hebrew Bible where the words "and you shall love" occur. So of course Jesus interprets them together, by putting them on the same level. The lawyer can only admire his skill in interpretation, with an admiration no doubt enhanced by the fact that this skill comes from an uneducated Galilean: "The scribe said to him, 'Well spoken, teacher; what you have said is true'" (*Mk* 12:32).

The parable of the Last Judgement in Matthew does no more than apply that teaching in one of the most brilliant tableaux of the Gospel. No longer is the man Jesus being interrogated by and returning an answer to a lawyer. The divine Jesus is seated on his heavenly throne and surrounded by *his* own angels – only God has angels attending upon him. The principle of judgement is the second commandment, equal to the first, and Jesus is seen with split vision not only on his throne of glory but in the poor and disadvantaged whom we meet every day. Lent is the time to look ahead and make use of the time lapse before the end.

Action:

Be especially aware, day by day, of those six special classes: hungry, thirsty, a stranger, lacking clothes, sick or in prison. Which can I help today?

Tuesday

Do not be like them; your Father knows what you need before you ask him. So you should pray like this:

"Our Father in heaven,
may your name be held holy,
your kingdom come,
your will be done,
on earth as in heaven." (Mt 6:8-10)

Readings: *Is* 55:10-11; *Mt* 6:7-15

✠

If we take a survey of the passages of Scripture which the Church has put before us in this First Week of Lent we can see the basic emphases of Christian life over which they range. It is as though a piledriver was being moved around, setting up the basic foundations for the pillars to support the whole building. So on Ash Wednesday we were told that it is all between ourselves and God: our Father sees what is done in secret and will reward it. On Thursday came the message of the Passion of Jesus, our model and inspiration; no Christian life can even begin without a consciousness of the self-giving of Jesus in his Passion and its acceptance by God, shown in the Resurrection. Friday brought the joyful message of the bridegroom as a background to sustain us in difficulty. Saturday wiped away any pretensions to perfection or even success on our part, for Jesus' preferred company was disreputable sinners and unclean tax collectors; if we want to be part of his company we need only to show him our wounds. Then Monday gave us the practical lesson of how to use our resources to help any who are in various kinds of need. Today, with the Lord's Prayer, we turn away from external activities to prayer and our basic relationship to God.

The prayer falls into two halves, the first half consisting of three petitions about the recognition of God in the world. In this half, a welcome for the Kingship of God is central, flanked by two equivalent ways of putting it, reverence for the Name or power of God and accomplishment of his will. The prayers on either side of the middle petition make explicit two principal ways in which the Kingship of God comes to be acknowledged. In the second half come three petitions for ourselves – for bread, for forgiveness and for protection from the allurements of false values. Is it the case again that the middle petition makes sense of the others, that forgiveness is the central value of the Kingdom and the prayers on either side are merely adjuncts? One could deduce that Matthew thinks so, for he chooses to stress this aspect by adding at the end the sturdy demand for active forgiveness as a condition of receiving forgiveness: we can't expect forgiveness unless we forgive others.

The whole prayer is introduced by the invocation "Father". We are so familiar with this that we can easily forget how extraordinary the privilege of calling God "Father" is. Surely the basic attitude to God must be fear and awe, perhaps tempered by reverence. A mere glance at the night sky and a thought of the distances and the expanding universe, especially by contrast to our own infinitesimal limitations, gives a conception of the otherness and power of the Creator. All we really know about God is that we can know and understand nothing. The Christian understanding of God, built on the revelation in Judaism and in Christ, is unbelievably different from other understandings of God. Think of the terror of a world ruled by an evil spirit or evil spirits as in some primitive religions. Think even of the basic severity of the Muslim conception of God as a judge, though a merciful judge. We dare to say "Our Father".

Action:
A visit to a church and some silent prayer around the concept of Father.

Wednesday

*The crowds got even bigger and he addressed them,
"This is a wicked generation; it is asking for a sign.
The only sign it will be given is the sign of Jonah. For
just as Jonah became a sign to the Ninevites, so will
the Son of Man be to this generation." (Lk 11:29b-30)*

Readings: *Jon 3:1-10; Lk 11:29-32*

✠

What does Jesus mean by a "sign"? In this Gospel passage
the listeners are told that no sign will be given except the
sign of the prophet Jonah. In Matthew's corresponding
passage this sign of Jonah is the Resurrection, for Matthew
adds the explanation that Jesus would be in the depths of
the earth for three days and nights, as Jonah was in the
belly of the sea beast for three days and nights (*Mt* 12:40).
However, there is another passage in Mark 8:11-12, where
the Pharisees ask for a sign from heaven and Jesus refuses
to give any sign: "Why does this generation ask for a sign?
Amen I say, no sign shall be given it." In the same way
Jesus complains in John 4:48, "Unless you see signs and
wonders you will not believe."

The most likely explanation, therefore, is that Jesus
himself understood "a sign" in the sense which the

Pharisees meant, as some catastrophic event from heaven which could not be denied. This sort of sign he will not give, for he needs a willing conversion, a free response. It is only after the Resurrection that the tradition develops, and the Resurrection itself is seen as this incontrovertible sign. So in the developed tradition of the first appearance of Jesus in the Temple in John 2:18-22 he promises them the sign, "Destroy this temple and in three days I will rebuild it." They think he means the Temple itself, and so do not understand. On this occasion John stresses that it is only after the Resurrection that his disciples understood.

So the saying in Matthew and today's passage in Luke was originally, like Mark 8:11-12, a refusal of a sign. By the time Matthew and Luke received the saying, it had developed with the addition of another phrase, "no sign *except the sign of Jonah*", which Matthew understands as referring to the Resurrection and Luke as the preaching of Jonah.

The preaching of Jonah led to the conversion of Nineveh, and at the final judgement the people of Nineveh will stand up as witnesses against "this wicked generation" because they recognised the judgement of God. So also the Queen of the South, who recognised the sign of the Wisdom of Solomon, will stand up as another witness. The failure of Judaism to recognise the opportunity is a major theme in Luke. Jesus weeps over Jerusalem when he enters the city because they have not recognised their opportunity (*Lk* 19:44). Again when he leaves the city on the way to Calvary he tells them to weep for themselves and for their children. The irony of the sign of Jonah is that Jonah, the prophet, and a member of the Chosen People, disobeys the divine command and tries to escape to Tarshish, while the people of Nineveh, wicked gentiles, respond immediately to the message of repentance.

Every speech by the apostles in the early chapters of the Acts of the Apostles ends with the same appeal for repentance and the massive response which this achieves. Only Stephen's speech before his martyrdom again marks the second rejection of the message by the Jews. Stephen massively underlines that this refusal is in continuity with the whole history of the Jewish failure to respond to God's call, and in God's plan this failure will compel the apostles to turn to the gentiles.

Action:

A time for repentance and a serious movement of conversion, reaching its climax in an Easter confession.

Thursday

*So always treat others as you would like them
to treat you; that is the meaning of the Law and
the Prophets.* (Mt 7:12)

Readings: Est 4:17; Mt 7:7-12

✠

One emphasis of today's readings is earnest prayer. Just as, in the first reading, Esther begged her husband the king for what she desired, so Christians must fervently ask the divine Father for their needs and desires. However, the last verse of the Gospel reading brings in the important moral principle known as the Golden Rule.

The so-called Golden Rule occurs in many different moral traditions. For example in an early-Egyptian papyrus, long before the time of Jesus, it is written, "Do not do to another what you hate to be done to you". In Judaism there is a famous story about the two Rabbis Shammai and Hillel, who lived a couple of decades before Jesus:

A gentile came up to Shammai and asked him to teach him the whole Law while he stood on one leg. Shammai sent him away with a flea in his ear. So he went to Hillel, who said, "Do not do to another what you do not want done to you; that is the whole Law."

Both of these are negative in form, whereas the form given in the Gospels is positive. This puts the concentration on positive action, a concern for the other rather than a reaction to what is done to oneself, and a positive care for the other. It is valuable to compare this principle of morality with other counsels in the Christian tradition.

The first is the Ten Commandments, inherited in the Christian tradition from our "elder brother" the Jewish tradition. These are negative in form, "Thou shalt not…", but they contain a whole positive world. Thus "Thou shalt not murder" implies a whole world of the encouragement of life. One who is true to this commandment not only refrains from murder but also encourages true life in all its forms. "Thou shalt not commit adultery" must also be viewed positively: adultery is the final moment when a marriage has broken down, so the commandment enjoins that the couple who have become "one flesh" have undertaken to bond together in such a way that their new life is one life in all their thoughts and desires, the partner being more important than the self. The positive side of "Thou shalt not bear false witness" is the positive demand for truth and honesty in all communication, in business, in information technology, in history as well as in the law. Thus the negative forms of these commandments carry also positive guidance.

In Gospel morality we have also the Beatitudes, which enhance the Ten Commandments. These come in different forms and different emphases in Matthew and Luke. In Matthew, starting with "Blessed are the poor in spirit", the emphasis is on Christian attitudes and states of mind, the states of mind from which Christian behaviour follows. In Luke the emphasis is on those in need, God's favourites, on whom God's special blessing rests, encouraging Christians to pay them especial care and attention.

Another summing up of Christian morality is of course the double commandment of God, love of God and love of neighbour, which Jesus put on the same level in Monday's reading. For Christians the Golden Rule does not stand alone.

Action:

Seek out some needy person who needs the emotional or material support which you most value yourself – either affection or material help.

Friday

> *For I tell you, if your virtue goes no deeper than that
> of the scribes and Pharisees, you will never get into
> the kingdom of heaven .... So then, if you are bringing
> your offering to the altar and there remember that
> your brother has something against you, leave your
> offering there before the altar, go and be reconciled
> with your brother first, and then come back and
> present your offering.* (Mt 5:20, 23-24)

Readings: *Ezk* 18:21-28; *Mt* 5:20-26

✠

The Pharisees receive a bad press in the Gospels, and
nowhere more than in Matthew. By the time Matthew
came to be written the only remaining Jewish group
was the Pharisees, who therefore personified the Jewish
opposition to Christianity. They are accused of hypocrisy,
especially in Matthew 23, but Pharisaic writings show that
they were well aware of the danger of hypocrisy – Jews
have never been afraid of laughing at themselves and their
unusual ways of behaving! During his lifetime, however, it
is not easy to see whether Jesus' disagreements with them
are hostile or friendly: he argues from Scripture in just the
same way as they do. Family discussions can be fierce
without being bitter! The Pharisees were so meticulous

about legal observance because they saw the Kingship of God to consist in perfect obedience to the Law. On many occasions in the Gospel Jesus differs from the Pharisees in his understanding of the demands of the Law.

It was in the application or interpretation of the Law that Jesus and the Pharisees differed, for there were traditional interpretations which the Pharisees held to stem from Moses, while Jesus teaches that, at least in some cases, the Pharisees treat as divine law what is no more than human tradition (*Mk* 7:7-8). Again and again he clinches his arguments by an appeal to Scripture, and even when he does not quote it on the surface, one can see that the scriptural text lies behind his thinking. It is the really important sayings and parts of Scripture that lie behind his teaching. For instance, when he says, "The Sabbath was *made* for man, not man for the Sabbath" (*Mk* 2:28) he must have in mind Genesis 1, the story of the *making* of all things, which climaxes in the Sabbath.

Today's Gospel reading introduces six occasions (*Mt* 5:21-48 – they are collected together, not all necessarily pronounced on the same occasion) on which Jesus brings the Law to perfection. In some cases Jesus is more demanding than the Law; on other occasions he re-interprets the Law; on still other occasions he goes behind the Law to the motivations which guide its observance. It is significant that the first and the last of these demands concern love. A first and last often serve as a sort of bracket to indicate the subject matter of the whole, so in this case indicate that all are ways of loving more perfectly. The first is about anger, which is a manifestation of hate, the opposite of love. The firmness of going to court against someone is an expression of irreconcilability, the very opposite of yielding in love. You can hardly call "brother" someone against whom you go to law. By contrast, the final demand shows the limitlessness of real love.

If we take seriously the greeting of peace at the Eucharist it can be very demanding, but all the more necessary for that.

Action:

Leave your offering at the altar. Forget everything else about Lent, but go and be reconciled to your brother or sister.

Saturday

> *Jesus said to his disciples: "You have learnt how it was*
> *said: You must love your neighbour and hate your*
> *enemy. But I say this to you: love your enemies and*
> *pray for those who persecute you; in this way you will*
> *be sons of your Father in heaven, for he causes his sun*
> *to rise on bad men as well as good, and his rain to fall*
> *on honest and dishonest men alike." (Mt 5:43-45a)*

Readings: *Dt* 26:16-19; *Mt* 5:43-48

✠

Deuteronomy is the fifth and final book of the Law, and ends up with a series of blessings and curses for those who keep or do not keep the Law respectively, beginning just after this reading. But, unusually for a Book about Law, it is concerned chiefly with love. This is why today's reading is chosen to pair with the last of Jesus' six corrections of or adjustments to the Law, which is also all about the perfection of love. Jesus stresses that our love must be perfect, just as that of the heavenly Father is perfect.

In the same way, the first great statement of Deuteronomy is that we are to love the Lord with all our heart, all our mind, all our strength. This command, called the *Shema* (which means "Listen!", the first word of

Dt 6:4-9), is repeated daily by every faithful Jew, as a sort of *Credo*, a basis of life: the principle by which Israel lives is the love of God. The Law here given is not constricting but liberating, showing us how to love, that is, how to be God's own people.

If we put together these two great statements about divine love, and our need and duty to emulate divine love, to make our love as perfect as God's love, it could do no harm to begin with some particular aspects of love drawn from Scripture in Pope Francis' letter *Amoris Laetitia*. This letter sums up the thoughts of the Synod on the Family, and the family is the basic focus of love, the wellspring of love, the place where love is seen at its most basic and also at its fullest. A first thought about family love is that it generates life. Francis relates the two Hebrew words for "son" and "build" (*ben* and *banah*): a child is clearly the product of an act of love, building up the family, and indeed the human race, as well as the child himself or herself. A child calls forth the love of parents in the continuous care needed, and in the anxiety to build up the child in every way, to encourage the child and take him or her further in the course of life, developing skills and talents. At least in the early days and weeks, the whole life of a mother is directed to fostering the child. In this way parental love is the paradigm of love, but still only weakly imaging divine love.

A second dimension of divine love imaged in the family is forgiveness. For many couples the sexual union is the total expression of forgiveness. No family is without offences, and between siblings and family generations forgiveness is the mode and template of family life. Without forgiveness there is no family, and it is in the family that we can be sure of forgiveness. This again is an image of the being of God who revealed himself on Sinai, after Israel's first act of desertion to worship the golden bull (contemptuously guyed as a "golden calf"), as a "God of tenderness and compassion, slow to anger, rich in kindness and faithfulness" (*Ex* 34:6). This is the description of God which thereafter echoes down the scriptures in prayers, poems and procedures.

Action:

If we need to know what is meant by our love being as perfect as God's love we could well start with the unconditional fostering of the life of others, and with unconditional forgiveness.

Second Sunday of Lent

Then Peter spoke to Jesus: "Rabbi," he said "it is
wonderful for us to be here; so let us make three tents,
one for you, one for Moses and one for Elijah". He did
not know what to say; they were so frightened. And
a cloud came, covering them in shadow; and there
came a voice from the cloud, "This is my Son,
the Beloved. Listen to him." (Mk 9:5-7)

Readings: *Gn* 22:1-2, 9-13, 15-18; *Rm* 8:31-34; *Mk* 9:2-10

✠

It will be remembered that the first readings of the Sundays
in Lent take us gradually through the history of the Chosen
People in the Old Testament. The first reading for the first
Sunday this year is drawn from the myths of the beginnings,
the covenant with Noah after the cleansing of the world
by flood. The second Sunday always recalls the history of
Abraham, and this year the first reading pairs nicely with
the Gospel reading of the Transfiguration, for both are
concerned with an experience of God on a high mountain.
The first reading this year also links with the second, for
Abraham's willingness to sacrifice his son Isaac is seen in

the Letter to the Romans and in the subsequent tradition as a preparation for God's willingness to allow his Son Jesus to be sacrificed: "God did not spare his own Son, but gave him up for the sake of us all". We are already preparing for the dire events of Good Friday.

The story of this testing of Abraham's faith is agonising, setting as it does Abraham's paternal love for his son against his trust in God, two ultimate values that should never clash. The story is told with a maximum of horrified drama, as father and son walk together towards the scene of sacrifice. It must be remembered that child sacrifice was well known in that world, and that it was not unheard of for a father to sacrifice his eldest son on the city walls to secure victory. On one occasion the Israelites were so disgusted that they lifted the siege (*2 K* 3:27). Is one of the purposes of this story to show that child sacrifice can never be pleasing to God? Did Abraham's confidence in God stretch to the conviction that he would somehow be delivered from the final stroke?

From this dark scene it is a relief to turn to the light of the Transfiguration. Here the emphasis is on the experience of Jesus by his chosen disciples as a more-than-earthly figure. The scene is full of symbolism. It is not explicit that Jesus is perceived as divine, but everything points in that direction. The glimmering or glittering white clothing is an apocalyptic sign of transcendence. Moses and Elijah are there because they both experienced God on the holy mountain of Sinai or Horeb (*Ex* 33-34 and *1 K* 19 respectively). The bewildered fear of the disciples suggests that their experience is similar. The Voice from the cloud, a symbol of God's presence, interprets the scene definitively, repeating the declaration at the Baptism of Jesus with the addition of "Listen to him!" Yet in Judaism the title "son of God" does not necessarily imply equality with God. In the prophets it is used of Israel, God's cherished son (*Ho* 11:1-4), and of the angels who cluster round God as his courtiers and servants (*Jb* 1-2). They share God's power as his agents and do his will, diffusing his powers as his agents but not his equals. We have yet to reach the clarity of the Fourth Gospel, though no angel is ever called God's "beloved son".

Action:

Make a special fuss of the family, as though you had narrowly escaped from sacrificing them!

Monday

*Jesus said to his disciples: "Be compassionate as your
Father is compassionate. Do not judge, and you will
not be judged yourselves; do not condemn, and you
will not be condemned yourselves; grant pardon, and
you will be pardoned. Give, and there will be gifts for
you: a full measure, pressed down, shaken together,
and running over, will be poured into your lap;
because the amount you measure out is the amount
you will be given back." (Lk 6:36-38)*

Readings: *Dn* 9:4-10; *Lk* 6:36-38

✠

The first reading is the early part of a long and fine prayer of
the prophet Daniel. It is marked by the consciousness of sin
and failure which is a characteristic of the spirituality after
the Babylonian Exile. The Jews were acutely and miserably
aware that they had failed and drawn upon themselves the
punishment of the Exile. They had lost everything they
valued, their city (God's own capital and dwelling place
on earth) and their king (God's representative on earth).
They had broken the covenant so often and so thoroughly
that their beloved Lord had no option but to send them
into exile amid strange people, strange gods and strange
religious customs. In so doing, God had allowed his own

precious Name to be despised by the surrounding peoples, as though he was a god who could not even protect his own people, whom he had sworn to protect and cherish.

In fact, of course, the Exile was far from so disastrous. It also brought renewal and a fresh start, a fresh hope. The contact with other gods enabled them to understand that their Lord was not simply the God of Israel but was God of the whole world, beside whom no other god had any currency. They learnt that they were not invulnerable and imperishable simply by being God's own people, but that they must respond as the Servant of God. Ezekiel expresses this in God's name, "I shall give you a new heart, and put a new spirit in you. I shall remove the heart of stone from your bodies and give you a heart of flesh instead" (36:26). They began to hope much more vividly for a time when God would transform the world by taking away all sin, suffering and sorrow, when God would be recognised by all people as the Lord and Saviour, when God himself would be truly present among his people in a new way, and all nations would share in that happiness.

It is also against this background that Luke is writing. Both Luke and Matthew are using the first Gospel to be written, the Gospel of Mark. They expand this Gospel, giving far more of the teaching of Jesus. Mark is concerned primarily to give a picture of the wonder of the personality of Jesus. Matthew and Luke have long passages of the teaching of Jesus which do not appear in Mark, and which must have been handed down separately, though in a tradition to which they both had access. Each of the inspired authors has his own way of handling this material, and also his own stylistic features. Thus Matthew has the saying "Be *perfect* as your heavenly Father is *perfect*" (5:48), whereas Luke has "Be *merciful* just as your Father is *merciful*." Then Matthew has "Do not judge", while Luke (who likes to stress a point with a fourfold rhythm) has "Do not judge…, do not condemn…, forgive…, give…". Luke follows this with another fourfold rhythm, "full, pressed down, shaken together, running over", before rejoining Matthew with "the amount you measure out is the amount you will be given back".

The most important variation is Luke's "merciful", instead of Matthew's "perfect", for to Luke Jesus is especially a figure of mercy, who calls the sinner and the outcast to repentance.

Action:

Is there anyone whom you need to forgive, to be merciful towards as your Father is merciful?

Tuesday

You, however, must not allow yourselves to be called Rabbi, since you have only one Master, and you are all brothers. You must call no one on earth your father, since you have only one Father, and he is in heaven.
(*Mt* 23:8-9)

Readings: *Is* 1:10, 16-20; *Mt* 23:1-12

✠

Today's readings constitute a vigorous attack on hypocrisy. The reading from Isaiah is a summons to the leaders of Jerusalem to appear in court before the Lord and justify their conduct. They are called "rulers of Sodom" and "people of Gomorrah" to stress that, for all their sacrifices and pious practices, they are no better than the leaders of those two most wicked of cities, destroyed by fire and brimstone. These two mythical cities serve as cyphers for everything evil. The land at the southern end of the Dead Sea is particularly barren and utterly inhospitable. Nothing grows there; no signs of life, no seabirds, no insects even survive in the salt-laden atmosphere produced by the evaporation of the enclosed sea so far below "sea level", notoriously the lowest point on earth. It is not clear what their final crime was, whether homosexual orgies or abuse of hospitality – leave it as the worst thing you can imagine.

In any case, the leaders of Jerusalem earn their titles by their outward show of religious practice unsupported by any real devotion.

Some decades later Matthew voices the same criticism by his sevenfold indictment of the Pharisees and their legal experts (of which we read only the introduction). The Pharisees were the largest group in Judaism at the time of Jesus, and Josephus, the contemporary historian, gives a more sympathetic picture of them than Matthew. They stuck together and supported one another. Sticklers as they were for exact observance not only of the Law but also of the oral tradition, they needed lawyers or "scribes" to guide them through the maze of obligations, often mutually exclusive. Should you replace an electrical fuse on the Sabbath? Only if it will save a life. What if I don't have enough light to read my prayer book? Should I collect prescribed medicine from the chemist who is further away than the permitted distance? If there are hard-and-fast rules to safeguard an important principle, there are always occasions when even the most observant practitioners will be tempted to make exceptions. Christian marriage is as enduring as Christ's love for the Church, but how much abuse must a partner endure before accepting that the marriage has died? What part should the individual conscience play?

Perhaps there are two related principal dangers. The first is that obedience to the letter of the Law may be used to block out the demands of true Christian love. The second is that blind obedience to the letter of the Law may prevent the formation of conscience. It is not always the case that "Man was not made for the Sabbath but the Sabbath for man" should be applied. Another danger, highlighted in today's Gospel reading, is pride in exact observance, and especially in the position of instructing others.

Action:

Gather up some superfluous clothes, books, etc., and think of who could benefit from them.

Wednesday

*But Jesus called them to him and said, "…and anyone
who wants to be first among you must be your slave,
just as the Son of Man came not to be served but
to serve, and to give his life as a ransom for many."*
(*Mt* 20:27-28)

Readings: *Jr* 18:18-20; *Mt* 20:17-28

The three great explicit prophecies of the Passion bestride
the Gospel narrative as Jesus approaches the cross. Today's
reading gives us the third and most detailed prophecy,
whereas the first one occurs in Luke's version on the day
after Ash Wednesday, putting the whole Lenten season
in perspective.

In arranging his Gospel Mark must deliberately have
intended the message that they too must take up their cross
to follow Jesus to be ever more pressingly in the mind of
his listeners, for each prophecy goes into greater detail.
Each time, the disciples fail to pick up the message; instead,
they seem to turn a deaf ear and squabble about their own
precedence. Matthew follows this arrangement too, but
here he spares the sons of Zebedee by putting their request
for the best places in the Kingdom in the mouth of their

mother rather than on their own lips. Matthew is always aware of the community which is to follow, and is aware that the disciples are to be the leaders of that community. Consequently he several times tones down the more severe rebukes of Jesus to the disciples: Jesus chides them not for their lack of faith, but for their "little faith" (e.g. *Mt* 14:31). They do believe, but not all that strongly, especially when the impetuous Peter has just had a dunking!

This prophecy of Jesus is today paired with the sarcasm of the opponents of the prophet Jeremiah, and the plaints of the prophet himself. Jeremiah was an unwilling prophet. Indeed to be unwilling is almost a necessary condition of being a prophet. At Moses' vocation Moses complains to God that he is "slow of speech" (*Ex* 6:30). Isaiah points out that he is a man of unclean lips (*Is* 6:5). Jeremiah, in his turn, pretends that he has a stutter, that he is a child and cannot speak – only to be sternly told by the Lord to snap out of it (*Jr* 1:6-10). At intervals throughout the Book he continues to complain, as here, about his hard fate. It is not surprising that nobody likes being a prophet, for a prophet is sent to correct the people and point out their inadequacies, not a popular task in itself. In Jeremiah's case it is worse still, for he has to prophesy that his own city, now besieged, is going to fall into the hands of the enemy. So he is accused of being unpatriotic and of undermining the defence. This will end in his being dumped in a dry underground water-cistern on minimal rations. Facing up to the truth is often unpopular; both Jeremiah and Jesus paid the price. One aspect of this is facing up to the truth about oneself, which can be very hard indeed, but must nevertheless be done, especially during Lent.

Action:

Is there anyone of restricted movement or bedridden or housebound who would be enlivened by a visit – better still with a little present?

Thursday

> *There was a rich man who used to dress in purple*
> *and fine linen and feast magnificently every day.*
> *And at his gate there lay a poor man called Lazarus,*
> *covered with sores, who longed to fill himself with*
> *the scraps that fell from the rich man's table. Dogs*
> *even came and licked his sores.* (Lk 16:19-21)
>
> Readings: *Jr* 17:5-10; *Lk* 16:19-31

✠

I once travelled overnight, arriving at a Christian institution as it was getting light in the early morning, and there, spread across the outside doorway into the street, was a man sleeping. He was lying on the cardboard of an old packing case, and had taken off his flip-flops (tidily beside him) showing me the scarred and gnarled soles of his feet. What was his story? Family break-up? Drugs? Alcohol? But there he was lying at the door of a well-appointed and comfortable Christian institution, and seemingly, when they opened the door to me, not to the surprise of the inhabitants. It gave me a real 'Lazarus' feeling. What should I have done, a stranger in the land, not even speaking the language? It reminded me of a story of Cardinal Hume: one evening Mother Teresa dropped in on him at Westminster Cathedral and said, "Come on, we are going out on the Embankment." Out they went, and there, under a bridge, was a man crouched in a cardboard box, looking at a photograph in a book. When they bent over, they saw that the photograph was a picture of Mother Teresa. When he looked up an amazed smile spread over his face.

What then of the story of the Rich Man and Lazarus? The rich man was not all bad. He did nothing for Lazarus, but he did at least care for his brothers and want to save them from his own predicament. From our own comfortable situation we must always be haunted by such pictures. Luke's high-level grammar and vocabulary show that he was writing for a sophisticated audience, no longer the cornershop world of Mark but the supermarket world, where people understand about debt and banks and lending at interest (19:23). The Dishonest Steward merely cuts off the illegal rates of interest that his master was charging his debtors (16:5-7). The sums of money Luke mentions are larger: as they set out on their mission Mark tells the disciples not to carry coppers in their belts, while Luke tells them not to carry silver. Luke is acutely aware of the dangers of wealth and of the need to use wealth wisely. It is for this world that Luke gives us the parable of the Rich Fool who builds himself larger barns, and settles down to enjoy himself, only to lose his life that very night (12:16-21). Similarly it is Luke who warns against inviting to dinner only those who can repay the invitation with another. In the Infancy Stories of Luke we see precisely the reverse situation, for it is to the poor and the disadvantaged that the Messiah comes. The Baptist is born to a childless old couple; the Messiah himself is cradled among the cattle and greeted by penniless hired shepherds, far removed from Matthew's distinguished Magi in their caravan from the remote East.

Action:

Is there anyone I could help to get over a "bad patch", or to whom I could give something that shows that somebody cares?

Friday

Listen to another parable. There was a man,
a landowner, who planted a vineyard; he fenced it
round, dug a winepress in it and built a tower;
then he leased it to tenants and went abroad.
When vintage time drew near he sent his servants
to the tenants to collect his produce. But the
tenants seized his servants, thrashed one, killed
another and stoned a third. (Mt 21:33-35)

Readings: *Gn* 37:3-4, 12-13, 17-28; *Mt* 21:33-43, 45-46

✠

The two stories in today's readings are both about a beloved son and the plans to kill him. The first reading brings us Joseph, the cheeky young upstart who upsets his older brothers by his pertness so much that they take the first opportunity to get rid of him. Unexpectedly, the story results in the brothers being saved through his heartless revenge – or at least through its consequences. The Gospel reading gives us the story of another son of a loving father, who similarly saves his brothers. But this time the son is killed and the blame falls on the brothers. The stories are not really very closely similar, but Joseph is a forerunner of Jesus mainly by being the beloved son of the father. It is probably better to consider each story by itself rather than extracting a lesson from putting the two together, for each is richly narrated.

The story of Joseph is delightfully told. The self-satisfied young pup insults both his brothers and his father before setting off blithely, scuffing his trainers and playing with his mobile – and getting lost. Two earlier versions of this story are combined, not without trace of the differences. In one Reuben affectionately wants to save Joseph, puts him in the cooler and is distraught when he finds that Joseph has been kidnapped by the Midianite merchants. In the other version Judah spitefully arranges the sale of Joseph to passing Ishmaelites. Either way, Joseph ends up in Egypt, and will get his revenge on the brothers by tricking and tormenting them before fraternal love takes over and he breaks down and identifies himself as the long-lost brother. One cannot help feeling that Joseph is the same cocky prankster, who has not improved much in the interval. This sort of tricky one-upmanship seems to have been much valued in that culture; it appears again between Jacob and Laban (*Gn* 30 and 31) and between Tamar and Judah (*Gn* 38).

The parable which forms the Gospel reading is both direr and weightier, for it forms the central piece which begins the final confrontation between Jesus and the Temple authorities. It is backed up by a second parable, the rejection of the invitation to the wedding feast of the king's son, which also teaches the failure of Israel. Jesus had himself taken over Isaiah's parable of the vineyard of Israel (*Is* 5:1-7), depicting the degeneracy of the vineyard, and developed it, to stress the failure of the tenants of the vineyard. Matthew makes it even clearer than Mark, showing that it is the disastrous climax of the history of Israel: the messengers are gathered into two groups, representing the earlier and later prophets, sent by God to warn the people of Israel. The Temple authorities could not and did not fail to see that it was aimed at their stewardship.

What has this reading to say to us in Lent? The Church and its members – not only its leaders – are the stewards of God's grace. We are the People of God, and assume that we are on the right course. Is it really so?

Action:

Bring the grace and love of God to someone today.

Saturday

*While he was still a long way off, his father saw him
and was moved with pity. He ran to the boy, clasped him
in his arms and kissed him tenderly. Then his son said,
"Father, I have sinned against heaven and against you.
I no longer deserve to be called your son."* (Lk 15:20b-21)

Readings: Mi 7:14-15, 18-20; Lk 15:1-3, 11-32

✠

God's longing to welcome back the repentant sinner is
one of Luke's most frequent emphases; in this chapter he
gives three images of the divine welcome for sinners. First
comes the image of the lost sheep, reclaimed by the good
shepherd, to the immense joy of his friends. But Luke is
always concerned to show the equality of men and women
(the annunciation to Mary is parallel to the annunciation to
Zachary; Simeon is joined by Anna at the circumcision; the
raising of the widow's son pairs with the raising of Jairus'
daughter), so he parallels the finding of the sheep by a man
with the finding of a lost silver coin by a woman. One can
imagine her sweeping around in the semi-darkness, for
there would not be much in the way of windows. One also
wonders whether the party with friends and neighbours to
celebrate the finding would have cost more than the coin
itself! A celebration is not a calculation.

To these Luke adds the parable of the Prodigal Son, which is almost a paradigm example of Luke's writing. Luke's source for this parable may well be the same as Matthew's story of the two sons, one obedient, the other rebellious, but it is enriched by his own wonderful storytelling.

It is centred on a person, and what a person! A hero or an anti-hero? He is utterly selfish, insults dad by saying in effect, "I don't care whether you are alive or dead; I want my money NOW!" He disappears in a flash, spends the lot, belies his good Jewish education by working for gentiles and looking after unclean pigs. Driven only by hunger, without a trace of family affection, he prepares his pretty little speech, only to have it interrupted by a hug. No trace of anything like "perfect contrition".

It is going to be some party, not just a hog roast (or lamb chops) but a whole fatted calf, enough to feed the whole village. And the father is incautious enough to give the wastrel a ring, despite the fact that it would enable him to sign away the rest of the money too. Then we get the other curmudgeonly son – what a pair! – grousing at the "Welcome Home" celebration. Even when dad leaves his guests at the party, and goes out into the field to draw in the brother, he merely stamps his foot and shouts abuse at his father.

The character drawing is, as always in Luke's parables, exquisite. Unlike Matthew's characters, which are monotone, either good or bad, Luke's are mixed characters, with enough good to be attractive, but enough bad to be like ourselves. This story brings home the delighted welcome which God extends to even the slightest sign of repentance. The elder brother puts the seal on it by illustrating Jesus' saying, "It is not the healthy who need the doctor but the sick" (*Mk* 2:17).

Action:

Would a small gift or token nourish the love between yourself and someone with whom you have recently had a disagreement?

Third Sunday of Lent

*Just before the Jewish Passover Jesus went up to
Jerusalem, and in the Temple he found people selling
cattle and sheep and pigeons, and the money changers
sitting at their counters there. Making a whip out of
some cord, he drove them all out of the Temple, cattle
and sheep as well, scattered the money changers'
coins, knocked their tables over.* (Jn 2:13-15a)

Readings: *Ex* 20:1-17; *1 Co* 1:22-25; *Jn* 2:13-25

✠

We have already noted that the first readings on Sundays in
Lent are working through the history of Israel as told in the
Old Testament, advancing week by week: before Abraham,
Abraham, now Moses. The reading for the Moses period
is the all-important Ten Commandments. We have already
(on Thursday of the First Week) given suggestions about
viewing these as a framework for life rather than merely
negatively ("Do not").

There are, however, other important aspects of the
Ten Commandments story as a whole. The importance
for Israel of the Sinai experience was that on Sinai God

made Israel his very own people, transforming them from a gaggle of runaway slaves into the People of God. The experience of God or meeting with God on the Holy Mountain is described in terms of thunder, lightning and earthquake, powerful and disorienting or – in this case – re-orienting experiences. If they were to be God's people they must behave in a way compatible with this, and form a holy society dependent on God and honouring God. This is set out in terms of an alliance or covenant by which a powerful overlord takes on a subsidiary group of people. Such alliances and their terms were common and familiar at the time, and would have been understood by the Hebrews.

These conditions of alliance are set out in the Books of the Pentateuch, and their nucleus is the Ten Commandments. These are basically the guidelines for a fair and supportive society whose overlord is God. The rules for behaviour in this society are important, but most important of all are the conditions which recognise and preserve the holiness of God. They were treasured by Israel, and it was a joy for Israel to observe them, not only as the terms of the alliance, but also because their observance was a loving response to God's loving choice of them to be his people, and most of all because this way of life revealed the nature of their God and Lord.

The Gospel reading is the first of three Sunday readings from the Gospel of John preparing for the events of Holy

Week. In Year A the three Johannine Sunday readings concentrate on the great mysteries of living water, new light and new life that are celebrated in the renewal of baptismal vows at Easter. In this Year B the approach is more historical, focused on the reaction of the Jewish leaders to Jesus. In today's reading Jesus stakes out his position in Jerusalem: the worship in the Temple has gone astray and is to be replaced by the Temple which is his risen body. The significance of this saying of Jesus of course became clear to the disciples only after the Resurrection. In the first three Gospels the cleansing of the Temple occurs not at the beginning but as the climax at the end of Jesus' ministry. In John, however, after this scene, on each of Jesus' visits to Jerusalem, the Temple authorities are thirsting to arrest him, but cannot do so until he is ready. In the Johannine Passion narrative Jesus is in charge, and nothing can take place, even his death, until Jesus has given his consent.

Action:

*Make an act of special reverence to express
that the Church is the dwelling of God.*

Monday

> *And he went on, "I tell you solemnly, no prophet is ever*
> *accepted in his own country. There were many widows*
> *in Israel, I can assure you, in Elijah's day, when heaven*
> *remained shut for three years and six months and*
> *a great famine raged throughout the land."* (Lk 4:24-25)

Readings: 2 K 5:1-15; Lk 4:24-30

✠

The story in the first reading is part of the background
to the Gospel reading. The Gospel reading forms Jesus'
initial proclamation in the synagogue at Nazareth, a sort
of manifesto, corresponding to the Sermon on the Mount
in Matthew. Luke takes the scene of the expulsion of Jesus
from his hometown, puts it a little earlier, and makes it the
scene of his programmatic announcement of his mission,
a mission to the gentiles. This infuriates his listeners so
much that they plan to throw him off the cliff. Luke wrote
both his Gospel and the Acts of the Apostles for gentiles,
making clear the shocking truth that Jesus brings salvation
not only to the Jews but also to the gentiles. It is rather
like the hoary old Catholic story of St Peter showing
a Protestant round heaven, pointing at a high wall and
telling the Protestant to keep quiet because the Catholics

behind the wall think they are the only people in heaven. This was a real point of contention in the first generation of Christianity. If Jesus was the Messiah of Judaism, was it not logical to continue treasuring everything about Judaism? Couldn't Christianity just build on Judaism and keep all its sacred customs? Change is always difficult for some people, and perhaps especially in religion.

The incidents to which Jesus here refers are taken from the Books of Kings to show that the mission of the prophets Elijah and Elisha were to gentiles as well as to the Chosen People. Luke often depicts Jesus as a prophet; when he raises the son of the Widow of Nain the people exclaim, "A great prophet has risen among us, and God has visited his people" (*Lk* 7:16), and Luke's depiction of Christ's Ascension is modelled on Elijah being carried off to heaven in a fiery chariot (*2 K* 2:11). A prophet is sent to draw people back to the true service of God, and this was a central part of the mission of Jesus.

Both are stories of faith in the prophet's word shown by gentiles when the people of Israel would not accept it. Elijah was fleeing from the idolatrous Queen Jezebel, who set about eliminating the prophets of Israel. When he reached Zarephath in what is now Lebanon he asked a widow for food and drink. When she replied that she had not enough for herself and her son, he insisted and she trusted him, giving him what remained of her food supplies. She was rewarded in that her meagre supplies never ran out: "jar of meal was not spent, nor jug of oil emptied" (*1 K* 17:16). Similarly the king of Israel thought Elisha could never cure of leprosy the Aramaean general sent by his king, but directed him to Elisha all the same. The general arrived in his Humvee outside Elisha's hut, at which Elisha did not even come out, but simply called through the door that he should wash in the muddy little Jordan. After a bit of extra persuasion he did so, "and his flesh became as clean as the flesh of a little child" (*2 K* 5:14).

Action:

As Naaman washed in the Jordan, is there any service you could do for a hampered neighbour – something like washing!

Tuesday

Peter went up to Jesus and said, "Lord, how often must I forgive my brother if he wrongs me? As often as seven times?" Jesus answered, "Not seven, I tell you, but seventy-seven times." (Mt 18:21-22)

Readings: *Dn 3:25, 34-43; Mt 18:21-35*

Matthew is a careful and highly organised teacher. The author of the first Gospel to be written, Mark, concentrates on the personality of Jesus and the gradual discovery that he is the Messiah, but does not go into much detail about the moral teaching of Jesus. Matthew and Luke fill this void, probably using a record of sayings of the Lord which was accessible to both of them independently and has now disappeared. Matthew organised this into five blocks of teaching, of which the fourth is chapter 18 on how the community of Jesus should live together.

The most important point, in the centre of the chapter (v. 19-20), is that Christ is present in the community. This is stressed throughout the Gospel, first with the name given to Jesus by the angel, *Emmanuel*, which is the Hebrew for "God with us" (1:23); Jesus is the divine presence among us. This is stressed also at the very end of the Gospel, where the risen Christ, as the Son of Man, to whom all power in heaven and earth has been given (*Dn* 7:13), sends out his disciples, promising to be with them for all time till the end of the world. The same teaching is at the heart of the community discourse in Matthew: "where two or three are gathered together in my name, there am I among them" (18:20).

The chapter starts on the optimistic note that disciples must be as little children (v. 1-4). But in what way? Is it innocence? Little experience of children is needed to know that children can be just as devious, selfish and cruel as anyone else. Simplicity? No, the child's world can be very complicated and especially muddled. For me, two characteristic qualities stand out: an openness to learn and an awareness of often being wrong. Children are far more willing to learn and far less worried than adults about making mistakes. Hopefully, of course, adults have learnt a little and do make fewer mistakes than children. If this interpretation is correct it throws light on the next section, the dire consequences (into the sea with a millstone round your neck) of putting obstacles in the way of children or leading them astray – precisely because they are easily led.

This is then followed by the duty to do the opposite, the joy in heaven when a stray is found and led back to the fold (v. 12-14). In this context the emphasis of this saying is slightly different from that given by Luke 15:3-7: there the emphasis is on the joy of repentance, whereas here, in the community discourse, it is on the duty to search for the lost sheep.

There follows a little passage about procedures for sorting out grievances, a process which is exactly shared by the rules laid down for the community of the Dead Sea Scrolls:

1. Have it out – don't leave it to fester.

2. If that doesn't work, bring in some trusted witnesses.

3. If that still doesn't work, as a last resort put it to the community.

The fact that it doesn't always work is stressed by the long parable which forms today's Gospel: the last and final resort of any community life is forgiveness. That is the mode of any community life. Seven is the number of perfection; seventy-seven (or seventy times seven) is infinity.

Action:

Forgiveness is best cemented by a gratuitous extra act of kindness – just to show for sure that you mean it.

Wednesday

Do not imagine that I have come to abolish the Law
or the Prophets. I have come not to abolish but to
complete them. I tell you solemnly, till heaven and
earth disappear, not one dot, not one little stroke,
shall disappear from the Law until its purpose
is achieved. (Mt 5:17-18)

Readings: *Dt* 4:1, 5-9; *Mt* 5:17-19

✠

There is a considerable danger of confusion here: both
readings for today praise the person who keeps and teaches
the Law. Yet Jesus, in the next verses of Matthew, sets
about supplementing it and actually changing it. Do we
have to obey the Law or not? Poor St Peter was confused
too: in his pre-prandial snooze on the roof at Jaffa he saw
a sheet let down, containing all kinds of forbidden foods
(*Ac* 10:10). He was profoundly scandalised when told to
slaughter and eat them. In Mark 7:19 Jesus "declared all
foods clean", but Matthew 15:10 pointedly leaves out
this phrase. The problem was aired on Friday of the First
Week. The solution lies in the Matthaean phrase "until its
purpose is fulfilled". In Matthew 3:15 the same phrase is
used at the Baptism of Jesus when Jesus submits to John
the Baptist with the words "thus it is fitting that we should

fulfil all justice". The Letter to the Romans is full of the same concept; Romans 4 is a meditation on how Abraham was justified by faith. What is this justice?

Primarily, justice is a quality in God. In human terms justice is adherence to a law, but in God this cannot be the case: God does not obey laws. In the Bible the meaning of a term is often best seen by its use in parallels ("O God, come to my *assistance* // O Lord, make haste to *help* me"). In the Bible again and again God's justice is put in parallel with his saving help: "My *justice* is suddenly approaching // my *salvation* appears" (*Is* 51:6). It is a saving concept, and is often translated "saving justice" or even simply "salvation". There is only one "law" which God can obey, and that is the promises he has made to Israel. So God exercises his "justice" by saving Israel in accordance with his promises. There is no single concept like this in modern thought outside the Bible, which includes both fidelity and saving power. So in God it is often rendered by a special word, not in general use, "righteousness". In modern English, "righteous" or "self-righteous" is a stern concept; it means consciousness of strict adherence to a moral code. This is not the sense of the righteousness of God; we cling to the righteousness of God in gratitude and hope, for it is our only hope of salvation. Abraham was *righteoused* (that is, saved) by his faith and trust in God's righteousness – this is the message which is being taught all over the meditation on Abraham's righteousness in Romans 4. This means that he was put in a position of salvation.

So human righteousness is not something which can be earned or built up, so that I can become righteous by my exemplary behaviour. I can only share in the righteousness of God by embracing the saving gift of the God who made these promises to Israel. It is tempting to talk about "being clothed" in God's righteousness. But it is not a pretty covering which hides a decaying mess. Divine righteousness penetrates the skin and heals the decay, making a New Man (male or female), a Second Adam in Christ. This is the "purpose" which is to be "fulfilled".

Action:

Share with someone else something you value, as a sign that everything we have of value is a gift from God.

Thursday

*Jesus was casting out a devil and it was dumb; but
when the devil had gone out the dumb man spoke,
and the people were amazed. But some of them said,
"It is through Beelzebul, the prince of devils, that
he casts out devils." (Lk 11:14-15)*

Readings: *Jr* 7:23-28; *Lk* 11:14-23

✠

The miracle stories of the Gospels must be carefully
handled. To what extent are they historical? No Christian
can doubt that Jesus rose from the dead, or more accurately
perhaps, that Jesus was raised from the dead by his Father.
Quite apart from the empty tomb, within about a dozen
years after the event the tradition is firm in Paul (*1 Co*
15:3-5) that the risen Christ was seen several times by
many people. But if this recounts real events – which it
does – there is no reason to doubt that the stories of Jesus'
cures and other wonders could be true. At the other end
of the scale is the story of today's Gospel, in which the
opponents of Jesus accept that he exorcised evil spirits.
The opponents of Jesus attributed this to partnership with
the Prince of Demons, but in so doing, of course, they
granted that Jesus did indeed have the power of exorcism.

At the time of Jesus the concept of "miracle" had not yet been developed. A miracle is something that simply does not happen and in the normal state of affairs could not happen. The concept presupposes a concept of the laws of nature and a testing which were quite alien to that world. Whatever a handful of sophisticated Greek philosophers and scientists had achieved, such scientific analysis was utterly foreign to the agricultural world of Galilee. There was a much more vivid awareness of the presence of God in the world, and the concept with which people worked was the wonderful power of God at work for those whom he favoured. The onset of illness was satisfactorily explained as the onset of an evil spirit, and release from illness by the superior power of God over the demon. It was not necessary to test out the happening in the way that miracles are tested out at Lourdes; it was enough that the power of God was at work in Jesus. This showed itself in many different ways.

Some scholars have tried to classify some of the wonders of Jesus as cures of psychosomatic disorders by the force of a charismatic personality. Some skin diseases which fall under the biblical definition of "leprosy", such as psoriasis, are stress-related psychosomatic ailments. Even in the modern world it is impossible to say what would be the effect of a confrontation with a man who was God. The Gospels offer us many and varied examples of the power of God at work in Jesus: the first disciples instantly drop everything and follow a stranger, notorious sinners are converted, despised tax collectors and gentiles find a welcome. These help us to know and understand Jesus. They are totally different from the magical tricks recounted in later non-canonical "gospels", such as Jesus turning a man to stone for bumping into him (and then, at his mother's bidding un-zapping him again); it is no wonder that the Christian Church rejected such narratives and that such "gospels" disappeared until they were excavated in modern times from the sands of Egypt. Such a person would not be the figure whom Christians revere.

Action:

Spend some time in prayer about an encounter with Jesus. What would he say to you and you to him?

Friday

> *Jesus replied, "This is the first: Listen, Israel, the Lord
> our God is the only Lord and you must love the Lord
> your God with all your heart, with all your soul, with all
> your mind and with all your strength. The second is this:
> You must love your neighbour as yourself. There is no
> commandment greater than these." (Mk 12:29-31)*

Readings: *Ho* 14:2-10; *Mk* 12:38-34

✠

Today's Gospel reading of the discussion between Jesus
and the lawyer about the most important commandment,
and Jesus' skill in using the rabbinical argument, were
considered on Monday of the First Week. It is now valuable
to put this discussion in its Gospel context.

It is one of four confrontations between Jesus and
various parties of the Jews gathered together by Mark
as Jesus' ministry to the Jews draws to its end. At the
beginning of Jesus' ministry, too, Mark presents a series
of four confrontations between Jesus and his opponents
(*Mk* 2:1-3:6), during which their hostility towards him
gradually increases until, already at this early stage, they
resolve to eliminate him. This resolve then remains as a
shadow throughout his ministry: the reader (or listener)

is already being prepared for the end. Now in Mark 12 the evangelist has assembled a second group of four confrontations, preparing the reader for the conclusion in the Passion, death and Resurrection of Jesus. First the Pharisees and Herodians (a grouping elsewhere mentioned in the Gospel only in the resolve to eliminate Jesus in *Mk* 3:6, at the end of the previous series of hostilities) try to trap Jesus with the question about payment of the tribute. Next the Sadducees attempt to make fun of Jesus and the doctrine of the resurrection to life after death. Thirdly the lawyer puts this question about the first commandment, which will evoke his admiration at Jesus' skill in the manipulation of rabbinic techniques. Lastly Jesus himself challenges the scribes, the experts in scriptural exegesis, to explain how the Messiah can be at the same time both son and Lord of David.

This final challenge is a reminder of the controversies in the Temple in the Gospel of John about the true identity of Jesus. More clearly in John than in the other Gospels, it is the identity of Jesus and his claim to divinity which constitute the issue in the final clashes with the leaders of the Jews. This will eventually issue in the "blasphemous" claim of his divine status for which he is turned over to Pontius Pilate.

The first reading from Hosea forms a preparation for this account of the rising tension between Jesus and the Jewish authorities. Hosea is one of the earliest of the written prophetic books (Elijah and Elisha were earlier prophets, but there is no written record of their prophecies). Hosea stands at the head of the Book of the Twelve Prophets, a collection of the shorter prophetic writings, and he is put there probably because of his record of the burning love between Israel and the Lord. God's love for Israel endures, whereas Israel's love for God is marred by periods of rebellion. In Hosea God's love for Israel is imaged as a husband's love for his unfaithful wife, and as a parent's unremitting and unrecognised love for a helpless child. Hence this final desperate appeal at the very end of the Book, "Israel, come back to the Lord your God", and the promise of a return to the unspoilt happiness and fertility of the Garden of Eden, "I will love them with all my heart, and they will come back to live in my shade." There is an agonising contrast between this loving promise and the growing hostility of the confrontation between Jesus and the representatives of Israel.

Action:

Invite for a cup of tea or coffee a lonely person, or someone who has suffered a recent bereavement.

Saturday

Two men went up to the Temple to pray, one a
Pharisee, the other a tax collector. The Pharisee stood
there and said this prayer to himself, "I thank you,
God, that I am not grasping, unjust, adulterous like
the rest of mankind, and particularly that I am not
like this tax collector here." The tax collector stood
some distance away, not daring even to raise his eyes
to heaven; but he beat his breast and said, "God,
be merciful to me, a sinner." (Lk 18:10-11, 13)

Readings: *Ho* 5:15-6:6; *Lk* 18:9-14

✠

David united the two separate regions of the Land of
Canaan (the Holy Land/Palestine) under his leadership,
and his son Solomon kept them together. But Solomon
used the people of the northern part of the land as forced
labour for his building projects, and in other ways treated
them as inferior. So when he was succeeded by a cruel
and dictatorial son, the northern part of the land broke off
and regained its independence as the kingdom of Israel,
with its own capital and Temple at Samaria. Both trade and
idolatry flourished, and with them oppression of the poor,
though the sacrificial ritual continued as an empty shell.

The prophet Amos was sent from the south to recall them to fidelity. He called them fat cows, lolling on their ivory beds and calling out for more drink. Indeed, in the ruins of Samaria ivory plaques from the sides of beds have been found, and they are decorated with Egyptian goddesses and pagan religious symbols. The grand palaces are built on the remains of bulldozed hovels. But the message of Amos fell on deaf ears and he was swiftly booted out.

At about the same time the prophet Hosea urged them to reform. He compared their love of God to the light cloud of a morning in hot countries, which vanishes as soon as the sun gets warm. They made protests of religious loyalty, but these sentiments vanished before they could have any effect. He pointed out that religious ritual is pointless if it does not express genuine love. Jesus made the same point to those who despised tax collectors and any others who were ritually unclean. The Gospel makes clear that he was actually drawn to them in their need. Three times the Gospel of Matthew uses the same phrase from Hosea, "What I want is love, not sacrifice" (9:13; 12:7; 23:23). The word here used for "love" has overtones of "mercy", warmth and sympathy for those in need, a real desire to help. It is the word used by the sick who cry out to Jesus, "Lord, have mercy." It has been said that the true basis of religion is the First Aid manual rather than the prayer book, but this is not true either!

Against this background there are not one but two points of contrast in today's Gospel parable of the Pharisee and the Tax Collector. The first is the self-satisfaction and pride of the Pharisee at his performance of his "religious duties", contrasting with the self-awareness of the tax collector, who ticks no boxes. The other contrast is the revulsion of the Pharisee at the tax collector; he had no evidence about how the tax collector did his job. Even parking attendants have been known to help mothers if the shopping trolley overturns.

Action:

Read the whole prophecy of Hosea and treasure the relationship between God and Israel which he longs to renew.

Fourth Sunday of Lent

No one who believes in him will be condemned;
but whoever refuses to believe is condemned already,
because he has refused to believe
in the name of God's only Son. (Jn 3:18)

Readings: 2 Ch 36:14-16, 19-23; Ep 2:4-10; Jn 3:14-21

✠

The first and third readings are full of the presage of the dark days to come, while the other aspect is given in the reading from Ephesians, concentrated on the infinite riches of God and the gift of God's grace. Grace is not – as it is sometimes represented – a sort of spiritual fuel, but is a relationship, the loveliness which God offers to us. The more loveliness we accept from him, the more lovely he sees us to be, and so the more he loves us. We are truly God's work of art, lovable only by the loveliness which he gives us.

But first we must listen to the disasters of the final breakdown of the covenant, that covenant which we have seen developing Sunday by Sunday during Lent. The Chief

Rabbi once said that, while most national histories are a record of success, Israel's is a record of failure. Indeed the history of Israel, from Joshua's arrival in Canaan onwards, was a history of Israel's broken promises, until finally God had no alternative to sending Israel into exile in Babylon. This was the lowest point of all, and from next Sunday onwards we will hear of the New Covenant and the painful learning process by which Israel was prepared for the coming of the Messiah.

However, the Gospel reading reflects on the reaction to Jesus, elaborating that saying of the Prologue, "He came into what was his own, and his own people did not accept him" (*Jn* 1:8), for Jesus was a principle of division. Those who came to him were not judged, for the Son judges no one, but people judged themselves by their reaction to Jesus. The Gospel of John itself is a record of people judging themselves and falling either side of Jesus. At Cana the disciples believed in him and saw his glory, but immediately afterwards the Temple authorities rejected his message. Nicodemus fails to understand, but eventually brings burial spices for Jesus. The Samaritan woman begins by mocking Jesus, but ends by leading her townsfolk to him. Some walk away from the Bread of Life, while Peter refuses to leave him, saying, "To whom should we go; you have the words of eternal life." The sick man at the Pool of Bethzatha and the man born blind accept Jesus, but the

Temple authorities reject him authoritatively, becoming more and more blind as they protest that they can see. The chief priests condemn Jesus for blasphemy, while Pilate proclaims him King of the Jews. We too judge ourselves by our reaction to Jesus, whether we can see the glory that is his as the only-begotten Son of the Father (*Jn* 1:14).

Action:

It is Laetare (=Rejoice) Sunday, halfway through Lent, so rejoice! And be sure to share your joy with someone else.

Monday

He went again to Cana in Galilee, where he had
changed the water into wine. Now there was a court
official there whose son was ill at Capernaum and,
hearing that Jesus had arrived in Galilee from Judaea,
he went and asked him to come and cure his son as he
was at the point of death. Jesus said, "So you will not
believe unless you see signs and portents!" (Jn 4:46b-48)

Readings: Is 65:17-21; Jn 4:43-54

✠

The final part of the Book of Isaiah was written after the
return from the Babylonian Exile, when the exiles were
settled again on their own land. They saw this return
as the symbol and foretaste of an even greater renewal
– "Now I create new heavens and a new earth" – with
plenty of rejoicing and long life. The return was seen as a
foretaste of the final blessings. The blessings themselves
were conceived in the form of the blessings of the Garden
of Eden, when everything was as it should be, without
the intrusion of any evil or disorder, no weeping and no
early death.

In the Gospel reading we have the story of the raising
of the son of the royal official at Capernaum, probably a

variant of the story in the other Gospels of the raising of the centurion's son. Whether he was actually dead or not, this was a sign of the gift of new life. The earlier part of the Gospel of John has seven signs, of which this is the second, and the marriage feast at Cana the first. The final sign will be the raising of the dead Lazarus to life.

All these are signs of a reality which cannot be depicted – or at least not with any clarity. The Isaiah reading is striking in that there is as yet no belief in life after death – just a longing for continued life. Belief in life after death was slow to develop. During much of Israel's history it was believed that the dead were confined to Sheol, in a sort of powerless half-life, an existence which was almost a non-existence, in darkness, where there could be no praise of God, and certainly no meaningful existence. Then a belief may be seen, especially in the prayers of the Psalms (e.g. *Ps* 40:11; 138:18), that God's love is such that human beings cannot be finally abandoned. Job clings stubbornly to the belief that "from my flesh I shall see God" (*Jb* 19:26). Somehow God will rescue his chosen ones. Belief in the immortality of the soul begins to develop, as seen in the Greek books of the Bible some 200 years before Christ (*Ws* 3:1-7), with full belief in the resurrection of the person during the Maccabean persecution (176 BC, see *2 M* 7:9). It remained unclear whether all would rise, some to their reward, others to their punishment, or only the virtuous would rise to new life.

The Resurrection of Jesus was therefore the fulfilment of a hope that already existed clearly in Judaism. The element about it which terrified the women at the empty tomb was that there was no idea of a single, individual resurrection. The resurrection was to occur at the end of time. Did the Resurrection of Jesus mean that time had come to an end, and that the new world was upon them? A truly terrifying thought; what was happening, what would happen next? The power of God was mightily at work.

Action:

What could you do to bring new life, new hope, to someone suffering from depression?

Tuesday

> *Now at the Sheep Pool in Jerusalem there is a building,*
> *called Bethzatha in Hebrew, consisting of five porticos;*
> *and under these were crowds of sick people – blind,*
> *lame, paralysed – waiting for the water to move.* (*Jn* 5:2-3)

Readings: *Ezk* 47:1-9, 12; *Jn* 5:1-16

✠

From now until the end of Lent the Gospel readings are
drawn from the Gospel of John as the tension between
Jesus and the Jewish authorities steadily mounts. It will end
in the arrest and trial of Jesus. This week the readings are
all drawn from John 5 and 7, both scenes of confrontation
in the Temple. Today's readings have also a special focus
on water. This, too, is in preparation for Easter. In Year
A of the three-year cycle three Sundays are devoted to
the mysteries of Easter as they feature in the baptisms (or
renewal of baptismal promises) at the Easter Vigil. The
first is about water, the symbol both of cleansing and of
new life. This is a rich symbol, for life springs originally
from water, and all living beings need water to continue
and flourish.

The Holy Land is hot and dry; water is a perpetual
problem. If you stand on the large raised area, built up for

the Jerusalem Temple by King Herod the Great, and look to the east on your right, you may see the Desert of Judaea. More likely you will see little but a heat haze. There is a little stream, the Wadi Kedron, flowing in that direction towards the Dead Sea; normally it peters out in the heat of the desert before it reaches the Sea. The Dead Sea is an uncongenial stretch of salt water, with plenty of other noxious and smelly chemicals too – no birds, no living things, no life; it is well named! Against this background Ezekiel's vision is thrilling: a fresh stream emerging from the Temple, growing in volume and fertility as it flows. Fruit trees with new fruit every month. The stream will even make it possible for fish to live in the Sea. Wonder of wonders, there will be fishermen all round the sea! It is impossible to imagine anything more enticing. This is the image of the new life which the restoration of Israel will impart, the life of the messianic times. Such is the promise which Ezekiel, the author of this passage, gave to the exiles in Babylon, far from their homes and homeland, deprived of everything they had ever valued.

Shift the scene back to Jerusalem, but keep the same problem: water. On the gentle slope running down from the north into the Temple there is an artificial reservoir to gather the water flowing off the hillsides for a short time after heavy rains. It formed one of the reservoirs for the Temple, which lay just slightly downhill from it. Surrounding the reservoir are five colonnades – or rather four colonnades surrounding and one across the middle, dividing it into two pools. This is called the Pool of Bethzatha, and part of the steps down into it still exists – the author of the Gospel knows his Jerusalem well. Around the Pool are still the remains of little healing shrines, for it was obviously a place where sick and disabled people came expecting to be healed. The practice may well have been superstitious, but Jesus makes use of it to bring his own healing. The symbolism of this passage, too, is baptismal, for the waters of Baptism, touched by the hand of Christ, bring healing and new life.

Action:

Go into a church, take holy water and make the Sign of the Cross as a reminder of your Baptism.

Wednesday

For the Father loves the Son
and shows him everything he does himself,
and he will show him even greater things than these,
works that will astonish you. (Jn 5:20)

Readings: Is 49:8-15; Jn 5:17-30

✠

Today's Gospel begins where yesterday's leaves off. The Jewish leaders showed no interest in the cure of the man who had been lying on his mat beside the Pool of Bethzatha for thirty-eight years, other than the fact that Jesus healed him on the Sabbath. It was as though there was nothing unusual about the cure itself. Jesus claimed that it was just as legitimate for him to work on the Sabbath as for God. It was legitimate for God to work on the Sabbath because babies are born on the Sabbath, when God gives them life, and people die on the Sabbath, when God judges them.

However, the issue next gives way to a most noble discourse in which Jesus' divine claims are set out in a way unequalled in any of the Gospels. The definition of the equality of Father and Son with which we are most familiar is that of the Nicene Creed, "God from God, Light from Light, true God from true God, consubstantial with the

Father". This is set out in the terms of Greek philosophy which are none too familiar today – "consubstantial"? It is a philosophy of 'being'. The Hebrew mind, and so the explanation given in John 5, works more in terms of 'doing', terms which are in fact easier for most contemporaries today to understand. A car is defined in terms of its performance, a tool in terms of its use, a mathematician in terms of problem-solving ability.

The explanation in chapter 5 is bracketed at beginning and end by a general statement, "the Son can do nothing by himself" (vv. 19 and 30). This will then be applied, but first an important explanation is given: "whatever the Father does, the Son likewise does". It is not that the Son imitates the Father and has the same powers, but rather that the actions of the Father are likewise the actions of the Son. Then in each case of the detailed exposition there are two statements, as though two sets of statements have been put together. So the Father has made the Son the source of life (vv. 21 and 26). The Father judges no one, but has entrusted all judgement to the Son (vv. 22 and 24). Honour paid to the Son is honour paid to the Father (v. 23a and b). In all these ways, the actions of the Son are the actions of the Father.

There are two other seemingly contradictory statements of the relationship of Father and Son. To the Jews in the Temple Jesus says, "The Father and I are one" (more exactly "one thing", for the word is in the neuter, so not "one person"); they take this as a blasphemous claim, for they take up stones to throw at him. On the other hand, to the disciples at the Last Supper Jesus can say, "I am going to the Father, for the Father is greater than I" (*Jn* 14:28). These two statements are compatible with one another, and with the previous statements, if the powers of the Father in the Son are understood to be derived powers, but still identical. So much for a dynamic rather than a static account of the relationship of Father and Son.

Action:

Honour equally the Father and the Son by praying the "Glory be" a few times in the course of the day.

Thursday

> *Were I to testify on my own behalf,*
> *my testimony would not be valid;*
> *but there is another witness who can speak*
> *on my behalf,*
> *and I know that his testimony is valid.* (*Jn* 5:31-32)

Readings: *Ex* 32:7-14; *Jn* 5:31-47

✠

The confrontation between Jesus and his opponents continues in the Gospel reading, which immediately continues yesterday's reading. It was a major puzzle to the first Christians of the early Church that the majority of the Jews did not accept that Jesus was the fulfilment of the scriptures, for which Israel had been being prepared for so long. In the end they concluded that God must have willed that his own people should not accept the witness, and they appealed for this to the scriptures themselves. Writing to the Romans, Paul is agonised by this refusal, and sees it as a continuation of Israel's stubbornness throughout the Old Testament. He insists that the Jews are still the Chosen People, and will be converted in the end. He uses the image of pruning and grafting a fruit tree: dead branches are cut off and new branches grafted in (*Rm* 11:17-32);

in the end the discarded dead branches will be grafted in again. But he sees that this does not work – you can't graft in branches once they are dead! So he simply appeals to the mercy of God: we just cannot understand the mind of God (*Rm* 11:33-36).

The Gospels appeal to the text of Isaiah 6:9. Mark 4:12 understands it as God's intention that the Jews should not be converted and be forgiven: "everything comes in parables, and they will look and look but not see, *lest* they change their ways and *be* forgiven". This is the straightforward reading of the Greek text of Isaiah, though Matthew 13:13 reads it as a consequence – "*because* they look and look but *do* not see" – though he quotes the same text of Isaiah in verses 14-15. The same text is used in John 12:40 and Acts 28:26-27 to explain the blindness of those who did not accept Jesus. Cardinal Ratzinger (just before becoming Pope Benedict XVI) said that the Jewish reading of the Bible was a legitimate reading, but just not the Christian reading.

In today's Gospel reading Jesus cites four witnesses to himself. First comes the testimony of John the Baptist. The New Testament only hints at the full power of this witness: the opponents of Jesus in the Temple, realising the extent to which John was held in awe by the people, were afraid of saying his witness was not from heaven (*Mk* 11:32). The Jewish historian Josephus tells us that Herod Antipas took John into custody not because of his affair with his brother's wife, but to prevent a messianic rebellion. Jesus had reason to put this witness forward first. The next double witness he quotes are the works of the Father which he himself carries out (vv. 36-38), that is, the power of God seen in his deeds; from different points of view these works are witnesses to Jesus and witnesses to God's work in Jesus. Finally comes the witness of Moses (seen in the first reading today), by which Jesus must understand the whole of the biblical witness through the ages. From the very earliest times, seen in Paul's double citation of the tradition "according to the scriptures" in 1 Corinthians 15:3-5, this was vital evidence in Christian apologetics.

Action:

Is our way of life such that we really are witnesses to the love of God made visible in Jesus Christ? Reflect on factors for "Yes" and "No".

Friday

Then, as Jesus taught in the Temple, he cried out:
"Yes, you know me and you know where I came from.
Yet I have not come of myself:
no, there is one who sent me and I really come from him,
and you do not know him." (Jn 7:28)

Readings: *Ws* 2:1, 12-22; *Jn* 7:1-2, 10, 25-30

In the Gospel of John, which provides virtually all the readings from the fourth Sunday of Lent till Easter, we get a real sense of Jesus in Jerusalem and of the growing opposition to him. John seems to have a much more real perception of Jerusalem than the other Gospel writers, mentioning several landmarks, gates and pools which have recently been excavated, the village of Bethany (where Jesus lodged with the family of Martha, Mary and Lazarus), and the festivals in the Temple (Passover, Dedication and, here, Tabernacles or Sukkoth). This festival is still observed, when Jews live outside in bowers of branches and leaves, a reminder of the temporary dwellings of the desert wanderings, and a reminder now that all life is temporary.

This stronger attention to Jerusalem is made possible by the time frame of the Gospel. In Mark (followed by Matthew and Luke) Jesus makes one visit to Jerusalem as the final climax of his ministry, beginning with the solemn entry as humble messianic king and the symbolic cleansing of the Temple, and ending with the rapid disposal of this messianic impostor. In John the cleansing of the Temple is narrated as an initial demonstration which colours the future ministry. At each of the three later visits to Jerusalem the authorities are thirsting to trap him, but cannot do so because his "Hour" has not yet come. This "Hour", first mentioned at Cana (*Jn* 2:4), provides the structure of expectation which pervades the Gospel. It delays the action (7:30; 8:20), is imminent (12:23, 27) and finally comes as the Hour of the Passion and Resurrection (13:1; 16:32). It is one of those typical Johannine ambiguities, working on different levels and deepening the mystery of Jesus: In what sense is the water provided by Jesus "living water" (4:11-15)? In what sense is Jesus to be "lifted up", physical or metaphorical, on the cross or to heaven (3:14; 8:28; 12:32, 34)? In today's Gospel reading do they really know where Jesus has come from? Like Nathanael (1:46), they may think it was from Nazareth; but there is more to it than that. The most provoking of all the ambiguities is the final word of Jesus, "It is accomplished" (19:30): His life? His mission? The message of the scriptures? The designs of God?

There are more ways of teaching than straight statement – witness the sarcasm of the first reading from the Book of Wisdom, expressing the envy and disillusionment of the world-weary wastrel. Unknowingly, it focuses on the very mockery imposed by the Jewish leaders on Christ as he hangs on the cross, and the very formula used by them in Matthew's Passion narrative: "if the virtuous man is God's son . . ." (*Mt* 27:43).

Action:

Do something to alleviate the suffering of a sick person near you.

Saturday, Feast of St Patrick

> *When Simon Peter saw this he fell at the knees of
> Jesus saying, "Leave me, Lord; I am a sinful man."
> For he and all his companions were completely
> overcome by the catch they had made.* (Lk 5:8-9)

Readings: 1 P 4:7b-11; Lk 5:1-11

Note: The Feast of St Patrick today poses a difficult choice: should we
reflect on the readings of the Feria or those of the Feast? There are also
two sets of readings proposed for the Feast, of which we have chosen one.

✠

Luke's account of the call of the first disciples differs
from that of Mark and Matthew. Mark, followed almost
exactly by Matthew, gives a mysterious impression of the
magnetic power of Jesus: a total stranger, he passes by
first one, then another pair of fishermen and calls them to
follow him. Without a word or a hesitation they simply
drop everything and follow him – a total, trusting response.
This is the first example of forsaking all to follow Jesus.
It may be objected that they did not have much to forsake,
but at any rate they had the family boat and nets, which
was their whole livelihood. They may well have had a
prosperous business, for in Mark's account Zebedee, the
father of the second pair, had some hired men.

Luke's account, however, has notable differences. To begin with, Luke puts the call rather later in the story. The disciples have had a chance to know what Jesus is about; they may even have heard him proclaim the Good News, and witnessed the power of God at work in him. He has already begun his mission of healing and has started speaking about the Kingdom of God. The crowd is large enough for Jesus to ask Simon to put out from the shore. Anyone living on the shore of the Lake of Galilee would know that sound carries better over water than over land.

Simon, not yet Peter, is enough under the spell of Jesus not only to put out the boat but also to start fishing again. Anyone who has gone fishing in the Lake of Galilee knows that fishing happens at night, and the boats put in at early dawn; to fish during the day, when a crowd has already had time to gather, makes no sense at all. You put out in the evening, wait till the fish have quietened down, and then lay out the nets in a large circle (as the Greek of *Mk* 1:16 and *Mt* 4:18 makes clear), ready to pull in the trapped fish. To go to all that trouble in full daylight is a real act of faith.

But the real point of the story is that Simon Peter (yes, he is a disciple now) falls at the knees of Jesus and declares his sinfulness. Again and again in Luke, like the Prodigal Son, you can't be a disciple until you have admitted that you are a sinner, or at least admitted your need: the tax collector at prayer (18:13), the woman at the Pharisee's house (7:38), Zacchaeus at Jericho (19:1). The same is true in the partial parallel of Peter's second call after the Resurrection: to compensate for his triple denial Peter must three times protest that he does after all love Jesus "more than these others do" (*Jn* 21:15). Jesus came "not to call the righteous, but sinners to repentance" (*Lk* 5:32).

The first reading from the First Letter of Peter shows what follows, the service of the good steward, speaking and acting to bring the different graces to others, as St Patrick did.

Action:

The moment for Easter confessions is approaching.
Take time for a preliminary examination of conscience.

Fifth Sunday of Lent

> *"Now my soul is troubled.*
> *What shall I say:*
> *Father, save me from this hour?*
> *But it was for this very reason that I have come*
>   *to this hour.*
> *Father, Glorify your name!"*
> *A voice came from heaven, "I have glorified it, and*
>   *I will glorify it again." (Jn 12:27-28)*

Readings: *Jr 31:31-34; Heb 5:7-9; Jn 12:20-33*

✠

Each of this Sunday's readings brings us to the climax of preparation for the celebration of the Passion and Resurrection of Jesus – each in a different way.

In some ways the first reading from Jeremiah is the climax of the Old Testament, which narrates the advance of Israel through history. On previous Sundays of Lent we have followed the progress of the covenant of God with Israel, through the stories of Noah, Abraham, Moses and then the disastrous falling away which crashed into the loss of everything at the Exile – that is, the loss of everything except God's fidelity to his promises. For in the Exile came a new opening, the New Covenant which was to be established at Easter; it would be both deeper and wider than the first covenant. It was deeper because the Law would now be written on the hearts of each one – not merely a tribal loyalty but a personal commitment. It was wider because by the experience of Babylon God was seen to be God of the whole universe and of all peoples, not just of the little territory of Israel and its inhabitants.

The Letter to the Hebrews reflects on and lays open the efficacy of the priesthood of Christ. The Temple sacrifices had sufficed to express Israel's devotion, thanksgiving and repentance to the Lord, but not to save the world. For this the prayer of Christ's sacrifice was needed. His entreaty in the Garden, "aloud and in silent tears", expressed his willing obedience to his Father in the face of the extremity of human suffering which he was to undergo. This obedience, rather than the actual bloodshed, is the clue to the Passion; it washed away and annulled the disobedience of Adam, the disobedience not of a single person but of the whole human race from time immemorial and into the future. For this no merely individual human obedience could suffice; only the infinite obedience of the Word made flesh could present the obedience of the whole human race and so become "the source of eternal salvation".

The Gospel reading is the announcement of the Passion in John. John has no equivalent of the Agony in the Garden, for this Gospel concentrates not on the suffering but on the triumph of the Passion of Christ. The scene in the Garden begins with the arrest of Jesus, and they cannot arrest Jesus until they have fallen to the ground to reverence him, just as at the end he does not die until he has finished his work. So the willing acceptance of the Father's will is expressed by this prayer, a prayer of obedience and a prayer for the glory of God, well before the Last Supper. Of course Jesus prayed before his Passion, and different traditions of that prayer have been preserved in the synoptic Gospels, in Hebrews, and in John.

Action:

What is the hardest decision you have recently made in obedience to God. Thank God for it!

Monday, Feast of St Joseph

*He then went down with them and came to Nazareth
and lived under their authority. His mother stored up
all these things in her heart. And Jesus increased in
wisdom, in stature, and in favour with God and men.*
(*Lk* 2:51-52)

Readings: 2 S 7:4-5a, 12-14a, 16; *Rm* 4:13, 16-18, 22;
Mt 1:16, 18-21 or *Lk* 2:41-51a

✠

King David was a complex character, but the reason why
he cannot be simply dismissed as a murderous rogue is
made clear in the first reading. He was certainly a leader
for whom people would die. He was pleased with himself
when he had settled in Jerusalem and made it his capital,
and more, God's capital, by transferring to Jerusalem the
ark of the covenant, the symbol of God's presence among
his people. Having built himself a fine house, he thinks
he will build a house for God too. But God will not be
patronised by this successful bandit, now king. No, God
will build David a House, a House which will last forever,
which will of course need correction, but which will be
corrected lovingly and never exterminated. In the dark
days that followed, this promise would be Israel's stand-
by and hope.

But how could Joseph be father of Jesus, who was born of a virgin? There are two interpretations of the scene with the angel-messenger described in Matthew. The first is that Joseph suspected Mary of impropriety but was magnanimous enough to suggest a divorce which would spare her blushes. But why then was he described precisely as "just"? Kindly, forgiving, perhaps, but not "just"! The other interpretation makes more sense: knowing that Mary had conceived by the Holy Spirit, he thought he was unworthy to compete, and should quietly withdraw. "No," says the angel, "you have a job to do – namely to adopt Jesus into the House of David and so fulfil the prophecy." This is precisely what Joseph does. The story reaches its climax when he names the child, for only a father names a child, and by naming the child Joseph adopts him into the House of David. This is certainly "just" in Matthew's sense of fulfilling the Law, for he fulfils the promise to David.

Apart from this we know little about Joseph. In Matthew 13:55 Jesus is described as the son of "the construction-worker" (not so precise as "carpenter"), one of several siblings. One way of combining this with the fact that Mary remained a virgin is to assume that Joseph had been married before, and these were half-siblings. In mediaeval times this was padded out by the fact that he appears nowhere in the Gospels during Jesus' adult life, so he was guessed to be an older man who had already died. In mediaeval mystery plays he is sometimes an old fool, a clown, set opposite the holy Mary. This is wholly without foundation.

Our only other fact about Joseph is that after the incident in the Temple Jesus "was subject to them" (*Lk* 2:51). It is fascinating to speculate about their conversations together, the construction-worker and the child who was God. Was the child funny, mischievous, rich in that staggeringly simple childish wisdom, a fascinating companion, full of surprises? Joseph must have been a person of striking depth and strength, for Jesus called God his Father, and he must have formed an idea of fatherhood from his adoptive father, Joseph.

Action:

Do something to help a mother!

Tuesday

So Jesus said:
"When you have lifted up the Son of Man,
then you will know that I am He
and that I do nothing of myself:
what the Father has taught me
is what I preach." (Jn 8:28)

Readings: *Nb* 21:4-9; *Jn* 8:21-30

✠

The Gospel readings for most of this week are drawn from John 8. Yesterday, had it not been gazumped by the Festival of St Joseph, would have brought the story of the woman taken in adultery, whom Jesus refuses to judge. Today begins three days' discussion between Jesus and the Jews in the Treasury of the Temple about Jesus' true identity. It seems to be full of deliberately obscure imagery and paradox on the part of Jesus, and misunderstanding on the part of his interlocutors. What does Jesus mean by, "Where I am going you cannot come"? Or "I am not of this world"? Or "When you have lifted up the Son of Man..."?

This last is given meaning for Christians by the first reading, the story of the fiery serpent lifted up in the desert, by looking at which the sufferers from poisonous bites were saved. Christian tradition has always seen this rather curious (even superstitious) incident as a foretaste of Christ lifted up onto the cross and saving those who turn to him to be healed.

Twice in the Gospel reading Jesus identifies himself by the phrase, "I am He". The two Greek words may also be translated simply "I am" or, in answer to a question, "Yes, I am the one" or "That's me". It may, therefore, either have a perfectly innocuous meaning or constitute a claim to be the mysterious figure who so identifies himself to Moses at the Burning Bush (*Ex* 3:14). Nobody really knows what the original Hebrew word meant, or how it was pronounced, but it may be connected to the verb "to be". It is perhaps best to keep to the simple explanation that this Hebrew name for God is so awesome and so intimate that it is never pronounced, rather like the baby-name which everyone has from their parents, to be used only in the closest family circle. It is usually rendered "the Lord".

The phrase is thus perhaps the most ambiguous of all the ambiguities of the Johannine Jesus. It may be a divine claim or may not. When Jesus comes to the disciples on the Sea of Galilee and so identifies himself (*Jn* 6:20), it may or may not be a divine claim, for only God walks on the waters; or it may mean, "Don't be afraid, it's me!" At the end of our present chapter (8:58) it is certainly a divine claim, "Before Abraham was, I am", which would otherwise be grammatically strange. The onlookers also recognise it as such, by taking up stones to throw at him. We may therefore understand the phrase as leading Jesus' audience gradually and gently along to the full claim of divinity. This further makes sense of the other ambiguities in this conversation, which lend a general air of mystery, and suggest that we are travelling beyond the borders of ordinary understanding.

Action:

Put a flower or other symbol of honour and attentiveness before a statue of the Lord Jesus.

Wednesday

> *Jesus answered:*
> *"If God were your father, you would love me,*
> *since I have come here from God; yes,*
> *I have come from him;*
> *not that I came because I chose,*
> *no, I was sent, and by him." (Jn 8:42)*

Readings: *Dn* 3:14-20, 24-25, 28; *Jn* 8:31-42

✠

The confrontation between Jesus and the Jews in the Temple now moves into another key. So far it has circled round two topics, first the witnesses to Jesus (John the Baptist and the works which the Father has given Jesus to do), then whether Jesus has the right to use the divine title, "I am He". This last topic will return at the end of the chapter and lead to the conclusion of the conversation with the accusation of blasphemy. Before this comes the final topic, whether these Jews can call themselves true sons of Abraham. Like any Jew, they maintain that they are true sons of Abraham, and then go back one further and protest that they are true sons of God. The vital question is what makes a true son (or child) of Abraham, whether it is racial descent or faith, to which the answer is that from the viewpoint of religion it is faith that matters and that the true children of Abraham are those who share his faith. Jesus argues that they are not true children of Abraham because they do not believe him when he tells them the truth, and do not love him (*Jn* 8:40, 42).

Lurking in the background of the conversation is the question whether they are slaves or not, a question which Paul treats in Galatians 4:21-31. Abraham of course had two sons, one by the slave-girl and one by the free woman. The slave-girl's son, Ishmael, was normally held to be the father of the gentile races, inferior and so considered slaves, whereas the other son, Isaac, was the father of the nobler and free Jews. Paul, rather wickedly and wittily, turns this on its head, pointing out that Jerusalem is an enslaved city whose children are slaves, whereas Christians are children of the promise, children of the free woman and children of the free, heavenly Jerusalem.

Paul also makes the distinction between the son and a slave, arguing that those who are still under the tutelage of the Law are no better than slaves. Freedom comes only with adoption as sons, at the coming of the Spirit which enables us to cry out "Abba, Father" (*Ga* 4:2-8). In the Gospel of John the role of the Spirit comes only later, in the discourse after the Last Supper. There it is not said precisely that the Spirit makes free, but that the Spirit will lead Christ's disciples into all truth (*Jn* 14:26; 16:13).

The freedom brought by faith is also the lesson of the Song of the Three Young Men in the fiery furnace, which provides the first reading. Their observance of the Law is not a constraint, but is free and willing, and sets them free from all constraint, free from the flames, free from the orders of the tyrannical king, enabling them to stand proud and confident against all odds. The reason why Jesus' opponents are slaves is that they do not recognise that Jesus is the fullness of the promises made to Abraham.

Action:

Read Romans, chapter 8, and reflect on the freedom of the Spirit.

Thursday

The Jews then said, "You are not fifty yet,
and you have seen Abraham!"
Jesus replied:
"I tell you most solemnly,
before Abraham ever was,
I Am." (Jn 8:57-58)

Readings: *Gn* 17:3-9; *Jn* 8:51-59

The passage from Genesis which provides the first reading is the third account of the call of Abraham, but the first to include circumcision as the sign of the covenant. The naming of Abraham is also significant on two grounds. Firstly, it shows that God is in charge, for only so could he have authority to impose a name, just as Adam gave the beasts their names and so completed their creation. From being vague, nameless forms they took the recognisable forms of lions, tigers, giraffes and the rest. Secondly, it gives Abraham a new nature with the new name, since a name is always symbolic of a nature. In fact "Abram" and "Abraham" are probably simply the same name in different dialects, but here "Abraham" is given the slightly stretched meaning of "father of a multitude", *Ab Hamon*.

The Gospel reading introduces the final section of the altercation between Jesus and the unbelieving Jews in the Temple, which concludes with the accusation of blasphemy after Jesus appropriates the divine name, "I am" (see Tuesday's reading).

Jesus also claims glory, conferred by his Father. This key concept of glory (*doxa* in Greek) is awesome and inspiring. It is properly a divine property. In secular language it means glory, human renown or reputation (*Jn* 5:41), something on which someone might preen himself or herself. But with the Johannine convention of deeper levels of meaning it indicates far more. When Moses, despairing at the failure of the Israelites immediately after the conclusion of the covenant on Sinai, asks to see God's glory (*Ex* 33:8), he is allowed to see God's glory only from behind, for no one can see God and live. Then Isaiah, in his vision in the Temple, is bowled over by the sight of God's glory (*Is* 6), and again Ezekiel is bowled over by seeing something that "looked like the glory of the Lord" (*Ezk* 1:28). So glory properly belongs to God alone, and is a terrifying and awesome sight. In the Prologue to John's Gospel "we saw his glory" is the summit of revelation at the Incarnation. By his first sign at Cana Jesus made his glory known (2:11), but the fullness of his glory is to be shown only by the Hour of his Passion and Resurrection, the two being seen as one single moment: "Now, Father, it is time for you to glorify me with that glory I had with you before the world was" (17:5). So the revelation of God's glory in Jesus is another way of expressing the divinity of Christ.

In the synoptic Gospels this divine glory which Jesus enjoys is associated uniquely with the second coming of Christ for judgement (*Mt* 24:30), and especially the scene of the Last Judgement, when the Son of Man comes in *his* glory with all the angels and takes his seat on *his* throne of glory (25:31). The exception is the Transfiguration, when the disciples glimpse him in his glory (*Lk* 9:32). These are true theophanies, when Christ is seen as God.

Action:

What would be the chief blockages to my entering into the glory of Christ if I were to meet him today? What am I doing about it?

Friday

Yet you say to someone the Father has consecrated
and sent into the world,
"You are blaspheming,"
because he says, "I am the Son of God."
If I am not doing my Father's work,
there is no need to believe me. (Jn 10:36-37)

Readings: Jr 20:10-13; Jn 10:31-42

✠

Holy Week is fast approaching, and for today's Gospel reading we have the final confrontation in the Temple between Jesus and his opponents there. The first reading reassures us that this is nothing new in the history of Israel: God's messengers, the prophets, have always been persecuted, and none so much as Jeremiah. In the scene of today's Gospel we have moved from the Festival of Tabernacles to another festival, that of the Dedication. This is consonant with John's theme that Jesus takes over, or centres in himself, all the festivals of Judaism: he has taken over the Sabbath by (like God) working on the Sabbath. He has taken over the Festival of Tabernacles by claiming that he is the source of the living water which was a part of the ritual of the festival. He will take over the Passover by making it his own Festival of the New Covenant. So now he takes over the Festival of the Dedication, saying that he, not the Temple, whose re-dedication was being celebrated, is the one who was truly consecrated by the Father.

However, the subject of controversy continues to be the same. In John all these long final controversies in Jerusalem concern the identity of Jesus, and more particularly his divine claim. The Jews put it most sharply by saying, "you are only a man and you are *making yourself* God" (10:33). This is of course untrue since he is not exalting himself, but throughout Jesus' claims he is acting as the agent of God, doing the work and the works given him by God, as he stresses in verse 37. The focus on the identity of Jesus is firm. It is not a matter of the legal disputes which took place (especially in Galilee) about interpretation of the Law; neither the scribes nor the Pharisees are so much as mentioned in the Passion narrative. Nor is it a matter of the disturbance in the Temple. This may have been important in the mind of the chief priests, especially if the arrest of Jesus follows so closely after it, as it does in the synoptic Gospels. In John's arrangement the cleansing of the Temple was positioned at the beginning of the ministry, now long ago. Whether in historical fact it was important or not, this is not the cause on which John's narrative focuses. The cause which bulks so large is the claim of Jesus to be God.

Even the little rabbinical argument to defuse the situation, about the judges who exercise authority as gods, is on the same subject. At first sight this argument seems merely to divert attention from the real issue of Jesus being called God. In fact it is an argument based on one of the processes of interpretation codified by Rabbi Hillel, the argument *a minori ad majus*, "from the lesser to the greater": if it was legitimate to call judges "gods" because by judging they are exercising the function of God, then it was even more legitimate to call "God" him who has been consecrated by God and is doing the works of God, namely Jesus.

Action:

Is there anyone who could even think that I am persecuting him/her? Can I dispel that illusion?

Saturday

> *One of them, Caiaphas, the high priest that year, said,*
> *"You don't seem to have grasped the situation at all;*
> *you fail to see that it is better for one man to die for*
> *the people, than for the whole nation to be destroyed."*
> *He did not speak in his own person, it was as high*
> *priest that he made this prophecy that Jesus was to die*
> *for the nation. (Jn 11:49-51)*

Readings: *Ezk* 37:21-28; *Jn* 11:45-56

✠

The two readings today are independent, not linked to
each other, but each most valuable in different ways. The
first reading, from the prophet Ezekiel in exile, promises
the renewal of the kingship of David – one of the very
few passages of exilic times to preserve the hope of a
king of the line of David. But what makes the reading so
fascinating is the shimmering between the shepherd being
the agent of God and being God himself. Who will restore
the people of Israel on their own land? Is it God himself or
God's shepherd, David? David is to be the prince, but God
makes the New Covenant with them. "My servant David"
will reign over them, but "I shall make my home with
them." It is fully preparing for the situation when God will
be their shepherd, but at the same time God's Son, who is

himself divine, will also be their shepherd. The prophet of the Old Testament, surely not fully understanding the implications of what he is saying, speaks of the coming of God to restore his people in such a way that he implies that the messenger and agent of God will himself be God. In the Christian understanding this already suggests what will later be known as the Incarnation.

The Gospel reading, as is fitting for the day before Palm Sunday, is the immediate preparation for the arrest of Jesus. It is a typically Johannine piece, expressing the paradox of life and death: it is the visits of the Jews to see Lazarus whom Jesus has raised to life (Bethany is 20 minutes' walk from Jerusalem) that brings about the death of Jesus. The movement is subtly but significantly different from the story in the synoptic Gospels. The decision to liquidate Jesus is not – as it is in the synoptic Gospels – taken after the arrest and interrogation of Jesus, but has been made long before. This is a prophetic gesture, inspired by the Spirit, on the part of the High Priest. Whether the High Priest was aware of it or not, the process of the condemnation of Jesus was the work of God, and the High Priest was the agent of God.

This explains many details. In the Johannine account of the arrest of Jesus (18:3) there is not merely a bunch of Temple guards but a detachment of auxiliary soldiers. This implies that the governor is already involved, and has already been brought in by the High Priest. Their residences in Jerusalem were adjacent to each other (now the citadel at the Jaffa Gate and the Headquarters of the Jerusalem Police). As governor and High Priest, Pontius Pilate and Caiaphas were in office for ten years together; they must have consulted together when the governor came up to Jerusalem for the festival: "Is there anything I ought to know?" This explains why in John there is no interrogation of Jesus before the High Priest's council, but only a meeting between Jesus and Annas, the High Priest's influential father-in-law. The matter was already decided.

Action:

Jesus was unfairly condemned. Do I need to revise any judgements I have made about others, and even set about making reparation?

Passion Sunday

But Jesus gave a loud cry and breathed his last. And the veil of the Temple was torn in two from top to bottom. The centurion, who was standing in front of him, had seen how he had died, and he said, "In truth this man was a son of God." (Mk 15:37-39)

Readings: *Mk* 14:1-15:47

Note: The celebration of the Eucharist today begins with the commemoration of Jesus' entry into Jerusalem a few days before his arrest, when he is greeted as the king-messiah. In this year, this story may be read in either Mark's or John's account (*Mk* 11:1-10 or *Jn* 12:12-16). Mark's account is the simplest of those given by the four Gospels. It speaks not of large crowds, but only of "many people" and "those who went ahead and behind". John's account makes clear that, at the time, the disciples did not really understand the significance of the event, but came to see it fully only under the influence of the Spirit.

For the Gospel reading at the Eucharist itself, in this the second year of the three-year cycle we read the Passion narrative according to Mark. It is the earliest full account. Before that, we have only the traditional résumé given by Paul that "Christ died for our sins, in accordance with the scriptures" (*1 Co* 15:3). An important independent witness is the Jewish historian Josephus, who says that "at the instigation of the leading men among us Jesus was condemned by Pontius Pilate to be crucified" (*Antiquities of the Jews*, 18:3). Pilate must bear the responsibility for passing the death sentence, but how much was he manipulated by the leaders of the Jews? Crucifixion was a barbaric torture which horrified even the hardy Romans. Mark concentrates more on the significance than on the material details.

Like Paul, Mark stresses that the death of Jesus fulfilled the scriptures. Repeatedly he shows that the events fulfil particular scriptural passages, for example the flight of the disciples and the darkness at noon (*Am* 2:16; 8:9), the silence of Jesus and the spitting of his captors (*Is* 50:6; 53:7). Particularly, the psalms are fulfilled: the prayer of Jesus (*Ps* 42 [41]:5); the false witnesses (*Ps* 35 [34]:11); the division of Jesus' clothes, the mockery and his final prayer (*Ps* 22 [21]:18, 7, 1). This shows that it was not by any human design that this happened; it was all according to the will of God expressed in the scriptures.

Secondly, it is for his claim to be Son of God that Jesus is crucified. For the first time, at his interrogation before the High Priest, he accepts the noble titles "Messiah", "Son of God" and "Son of Man" (*Mk* 14:61-62). It is the chief priests who stir up the crowd to insist on the death of Jesus. After his death, when, for the first time, Jesus is acknowledged as "Truly son of God" by a human being, it is by the gentile centurion; this is the beginning of the mission to the gentiles.

Thirdly, once again the failure of the disciples is underlined. During Jesus' agonised prayer they three times fall asleep (14:37-41). One of his own disciples betrays him (14:10). At the arrest they first oppose violence with violence and then all run away (14:47, 50-52). Peter, having sworn loyalty till death, three times denies any knowledge of Jesus (14:29, 31, 67-72). At the death of Jesus none of them are present, only "some women", and they "at a distance" (15:40); their failure will come later (16:8). Mark is both stressing the horror of the occasion and showing the challenge for disciples of Jesus in taking up the cross to follow him.

Action:
Finally resolve to give up one particular bad habit.

Monday of Holy Week

*Leave her alone; she had to keep this scent for the day
of my burial. You have the poor with you always,
you will not always have me.* (Jn 12:7-8)

Readings: Is 42:1-7; Jn 12:1-11

✠

In the second part of the Book of Isaiah, dating from the
Babylonian Exile, are four Poems of the Task of a Servant of
the Lord. It is unclear whether this servant is an individual
or a personification of the People of Israel, serving the Lord
by witnessing to the values of God's covenant with Israel,
and eventually suffering for them. They depict a servant
of the Lord, wholly dedicated to the Lord, and pleasing to
him, who will bring true justice to Israel and to the nations,
and will suffer hideously and die in the Lord's service, and
will eventually be justified. Whatever the original meaning,
Christian tradition has applied these songs to Jesus and
his mission. Three of these "Servant" poems are read on
the first three days of Holy Week, and the fourth on Good
Friday. It is most likely that Jesus himself had this task of
the servant in mind when he speaks so frequently of his own
task of service – "the Son of man came not to be served but
to serve" (*Mk* 10:45) – or says that the first of his followers
must be "last of all and servant of all" (9:35). The Voice
from heaven to Jesus at the Baptism echoes the opening

of the first song, "Here is my servant whom I uphold, my chosen one in whom my soul delights" (*Is* 42:1); this was the signal that his public mission should begin. So in a way these poems sum up the mission of Jesus.

There seem to have been various stories circulating in the Christian tradition about a woman paying homage to Jesus by anointing him and wiping his feet with her hair. In Mark 14:3-9 at Bethany a woman anoints his head just before the Passion, and Jesus interprets this as preparation for his burial (as he would not later be anointed for his burial). In Luke 7:36-50 a woman sheds tears of repentance on his feet and anoints them with oil at the house of Simon the Pharisee; Jesus praises her for her unbounded love. Stressing repentance contrasted with Simon's lack of courteous hospitality, this is a characteristic Lukan story. There may be some crossover between the different stories, for anointing the feet is unusual (it makes them sticky!), whereas anointing the head is more normal (the warmth then diffuses the perfume). This reaction of Jesus in putting homage to his own person before attention to the poor is unusual. Perhaps it is intended to counter the horror that is so soon to overtake him; it is certainly a useful reminder of the honour due to his person in every circumstance.

Action:
What special honour can I pay to Jesus as I prepare to commemorate his Passion, death and Resurrection?

Tuesday of Holy Week

"Lay down your life for me?" answered Jesus. "I tell
you most solemnly, before the cock crows you will have
disowned me three times." (Jn 13:38)

Readings: *Is* 49:1-6; *Jn* 13:21-33, 36-38

The Gospel reading for today is most of the narrative of
the Last Supper given to us by John, not including Jesus'
action in washing the feet of the disciples (reserved for
Maundy Thursday) and the discourses after the supper
(*Jn* 14-17). We do not know exactly what went on at the
supper. We do not even know for certain whether it was the
Passover meal. Firstly, the evangelists are not concerned to
describe to us the meal as such; they prefer to concentrate
on three incidents that occurred there, namely the betrayal
by Judas, Peter's insistence that he will not deny Jesus and
the Institution of the Eucharist.

Secondly, there is a difficulty about the date of the
supper. Mark 14:12 is clear that the disciples were sent
to prepare for the meal as the Passover lambs were being
sacrificed – that is, on the Thursday afternoon, in readiness
for the meal which began Passover (in biblical timing the
day begins at sundown – a relic of a lunar calendar, by

which the day begins at moonrise). In John 19:14, however, the crucifixion itself occurs at noon on the eve of Passover. One solution to this problem is that John deliberately put the crucifixion at this time for symbolic reasons, in order to make the crucifixion coincide with the killing of the Passover lambs, reinforcing his theology that Jesus is the Lamb of God. An alternative solution is to suggest that Jesus was observing a different calendar. The Essenes seem to have had a different calendar, which would put the Passover meal on the Tuesday night, though this has its own difficulties. A third solution is that Jesus, knowing that he might be arrested at any moment, chose his own moment for his own renewal of the covenant with his disciples. This has the advantage of putting all the emphasis on the renewal of the covenant, the New Covenant foretold by Jeremiah 31:31. This was the principal significance of the meal of Jesus with his group of the New Israel. Just as the Passover meal was a commemoration of the covenant on Sinai, so now the Last Supper becomes a sort of prequel to the crucifixion, in which the New Covenant will be ratified in his blood. Hence the importance of the Eucharistic cup.

This New Covenant is preceded by the depths of betrayal. The betrayer first shares a dish with Jesus, the most intimate expression of hospitality given and received (and in that culture the obligations of hospitality were particularly solemn and binding). The synoptic Gospels do not at this moment identify the betrayer by name; they identify him only as the one who betrays the most sacred expression of companionship. At that moment Satan enters into Judas and night falls (*Jn* 13:27, 30). With only a momentary pause for Jesus to give the new commandment of love, "Love one another just as I have loved you", there follows the narrative of Simon Peter's protestations of loyalty and Jesus' prediction of his failure.

Action:

Reflect: is my loyalty any better than that of the disciples?

Spy Wednesday

When evening came he was at table with the twelve disciples. And while they were eating he said, "I tell you solemnly, one of you is about to betray me." (Mt 26:20-21)

Readings: *Is* 50:4-9; *Mt* 26:14-25

✠

The day before Maundy Thursday is often unofficially known as "Spy Wednesday" to give it special status as the day on which we hear the Gospel readings about the treacherous arrangements between Judas and the chief priests. Speculations about Judas and studies of his character have been endless. At one end it has been suggested that the financial motive, and indeed all evil intention, was a later addition, and that he was originally merely "the one who handed Jesus over", not the traitor; he merely arranged a meeting with the authorities so that Jesus and the chief priests could sort things out, and that when this went horribly wrong Judas despaired at the catastrophe and so committed suicide. At the other end Judas is simply the symbol of all evil, lacking any redeeming feature. Between these extremes are such strange theories as that of the recently rediscovered ancient manuscript, *The Gospel of Judas*, according to which Jesus is grateful to Judas for enabling him to fulfil his purpose.

In today's Gospel reading financial greed is paramount, and perhaps also disappointment or contempt, for thirty silver pieces is the price of a slave in Exodus 21:32. In recounting the death of Judas, Matthew 27:5 concentrates on the thought of the betrayal of a friend, for the only suicide in the Hebrew Bible is that of Ahitophel, the counsellor of King David, who betrayed his master, and then committed suicide when his advice to the rebellious Solomon was disregarded; he also hanged himself (2 S 17:23).

In any case, it is perhaps useful to regard Spy Wednesday as the day of evil, the day when evil temporarily prevails. In sketching his own struggle against evil (or perhaps the struggle of humanity as a whole against evil) Paul writes:

> I do not do what I want to do, but I do the thing that I hate, for while it is open to me to want to do good, the power to do it is not; for the good thing I want to do, I do not do; the evil thing which I do not want – that is what I accomplish. But if I do what I do not want to, then it is not myself acting, but the sin that lives in me. So I find this law for myself, that when I want to do good, evil opens up to me. In my inmost self I delight in God's law, but I find another law in my body battling against the law of my mind and taking me prisoner to the law of sin which lives in my body (*Rm* 7:15-22).

We all know the moment at which we give in to evil: "The baby is crying – let it cry" or "No one will notice that the DVD is missing" or more simply, "I don't care whether it is right or wrong; that is what I am going to do." It might be that Spy Wednesday could function as the symbol of that motivation in ourselves, the very opposite of the love and generosity of Christ which we are to celebrate and commemorate in the three days of Easter.

Action:

Prepare for the Easter confession, really looking at the driving motives, the darker as well as the lighter spots in life.

Maundy Thursday

*When he had washed their feet and put on his clothes
again he went back to the table. "Do you understand"
he said "what I have done to you? You call me Master
and Lord, and rightly; so I am. If I, then, the Lord and
Master, have washed your feet, you should wash each
other's feet." (Jn 13:12-14)*

Readings: *Ex 12:1-8, 11-14; 1 Co 11:23-26; Jn 13:1-15*

✠

The festival on which Passover was based was originally
a nomad festival at the move from winter pastures in the
plains to summer pastures in the hills. Instructions for the
meal are given in today's reading from Exodus. In the
nomadic festival a fine lamb was offered to placate the
gods, so that they would not harm the rest of the flock; it
was eaten at the first full moon of spring, after the spring
equinox (21st March). Blood on the doorposts of the
tents was a sign that the offering had been made. Water is
scarce for nomads, so the lamb was roasted, not boiled –
cooking pots were packed, anyway! This primitive festival
was taken up by the Hebrews to commemorate the great
move from Egypt through the desert, and – most of all –
the covenant made in the desert of Sinai, when God made
Israel his own people. It was celebrated each year, and the

blood of the lamb sprinkled over the altar (representing God) and the people signified their union in the covenant.

This feast was taken up by Jesus as the occasion for him to make his own New Covenant, fulfilling the promises made by the prophets of a new covenant to replace the old covenant so definitively broken at the time of the Babylonian Exile. The first Christians continued to commemorate it in their Eucharists. Paul gives us the outline of this last meal of Jesus with his disciples; he himself had received it from the tradition, hardly a dozen years after the Last Supper, well before the Gospels were written. Jesus himself was the lamb who was to be sacrificed, and his New Covenant was sealed, not in blood sprinkled but in his own blood consumed. It was a "memorial" – that is, an effective re-enactment, actually renewing the act of dedication and union. In today's reading Paul is rebuking the Corinthians for re-enacting this significant moment thoughtlessly, as though it was an ordinary festal meal; they had lost the intention and the seriousness. They were no longer proclaiming the death of Jesus, no longer engaging themselves in the New Covenant. It is a dangerous thing to commit oneself to a new covenant sealed by death and leading to new life, but this is what we do at each Eucharist.

Jesus' extraordinary gesture recorded in the Gospel of John shows us the full meaning of what he was doing.

The narrative stresses that Jesus knew what was to come; he was showing his disciples the meaning of the events. By the act of rising from the table and performing the demeaning act of stripping down and washing the feet of his followers, his guests, he was showing the meaning of the dire events to come – Peter's horror says it all, but there was far worse to come. It was a pre-enactment of his great act of serving his community, the new family which he was binding to himself by this New Covenant, the foundational act of service in the Church.

Action:

Perform an act of service which will be appreciated by some member of the community.

Good Friday

After Jesus had taken the vinegar he said, "It is accomplished"; and bowing his head he gave up his spirit. (Jn 19:30)

Readings: *Is* 52:13-53:12; *Heb* 4:14-16; 5:7-9; *Jn* 18:1-19:42

✠

John's narrative of the Passion is different from that of the synoptic Gospels in important respects. Some of these differences are matters of emphasis; others spring from a set of different facts. After Caiaphas' decision (see Saturday of the Fifth Week), no Jewish interrogation by the High Priest, no meeting of a Sanhedrin to prepare a charge to put before Pilate were necessary. Instead John gives an interrogation before Annas, the ex-High Priest and father-in-law of Caiaphas. The trial before Pilate may well be built on the same incident as that of the synoptics, but in John it is highly elaborated for theological reasons.

The Johannine account is not the story of a condemned criminal being dragged to the disgraceful and tortured death reserved for slaves. Jesus is the majestic king, who proceeds royally to his triumph in death. There is no painful prayer for release in Gethsemane. From the beginning it is stressed that Jesus is fully aware of what is to happen. Before he can be arrested his captors repeatedly fall to the ground in an involuntary gesture of reverence at Jesus' pronouncement of the divine name, "I am". Jesus commands them to let his followers go, and is taken only when he gives the word (18:11). The humiliating elements of the other accounts, such as buffeting, spitting and the challenge to prophesy, have disappeared. Jesus is emphatically declared king in the three great world languages by the very man who condemns him to death (19:20-22). John even notes that the proclamation was publicly acknowledged by "many of the Jews".

Not only is Jesus king; he continues his role as revealer and judge as well. In the interview with Annas it is Jesus who challenges and questions the High Priest, reiterating his own teaching which he has given "for all the world to hear". Similarly at the trial before Pilate, Jesus questions the governor and shows his control, until Pilate collapses with the feeble evasion, "What is truth?" – a humiliating self-condemnation in this Gospel of truth. The judgement reaches its climax when the Jewish leaders, in a formal and balanced scene, condemn themselves before Jesus: he is enthroned on the judgement seat as judge and crowned – with thorns – as king, still wearing the royal purple robe of his mockery, while they deny the very existence of Judaism by declaring, "We have no king but Caesar" (19:15). If the God of Israel is not universal king, then Israel has no point or purpose.

The final scene has special significance. Jesus carries his own cross, unaided, and is enthroned on it – no agonising details of nailing and hoisting – between two attendants. There is no final psalm quotation of seeming despair (as in Mark and Matthew) or of resignation (as in Luke), no wordless "great cry" as Jesus expires. In John Jesus prepares the community of the future. In contrast to the other Gospels, Mary and the Beloved Disciple stand at the foot of the cross and are entrusted to each other's care to constitute the first Christian community, the woman and the man, the mother and the ideal disciple. This is cemented by the gift of the Spirit, as Jesus – with typical Johannine ambiguity – "gave over his spirit". Does this mean "breathed his last" or "gave them the Holy Spirit"? Only then does Jesus consent to die, with the words: "It is fulfilled".

Action:

Spend some time in prayer of gratitude to Jesus for giving his life for us.

Holy Saturday

*But we believe that having died with Christ we shall
return to life with him: Christ, as we know, having
been raised from the dead will never die again. Death
has no power over him any more.* (Rm 6:8-9)

Readings: *Gn* 1:1-2:2; *Rm* 6:3-11

Note: There is no liturgy of Holy Saturday. Liturgically it is a blank day,
while the world waits for the Resurrection. However, the Easter Vigil
on the evening of Holy Saturday has seven Old Testament readings, as
well as a reading from Paul's Letter to the Romans, and the Gospel of
the Resurrection. We will reflect on the first reading, from Genesis, and
on the reading from Romans, leaving the Gospel of the Resurrection for
Sunday itself.

✠

The story of the Creation as told in the first chapter of
Genesis does not even pretend to be historical. It is a myth,
which means that it teaches important basic truths in the
form of a story. The story form is obvious: it is shaped
by the seven days of the week, ending with the Sabbath
rest day, a rest day for God after all his work. This is to
show that the Sabbath-day rest, devoted to God, is part of
the very stuff and pattern of the world. Obviously it is not
history, for to say there were three "days" before the sun
existed is a nonsense. Rather the framework is logical:

1. Light and darkness, without which no one can see anything.

2. The dome over the earth, snuggling the earth into a gap in the vast, amorphous waters.

3. Fixed objects on the land: plants and trees – no movable objects in the heavens.

4. Fixed objects in the heavens: sun, moon, stars – no fixed objects in the sea.

5. Movable objects in the sea.

6. Movable objects on the land: animals and humans.

What are the important basic truths? Everything is dependent on God. Man and woman are special (God has a little consultation, a climax, the piece of poetry, "in the image of God"). Man and woman make a single pair. They are masters of the whole earth, fill it and look after it; they are naturally vegetarian: there is no place for any killing. It is not about what happened long ago; it is about the world as we need to see it today.

The reading from Romans after the canter through the history of salvation prepares for the renewal of baptismal vows which is the centre of the Easter Vigil. It must be seen as the climax of Paul's analysis of Christ's work of redemption. Christ's act of perfect, loving obedience to his Father in the crucifixion annulled the disobedience of

Adam and the whole human race. It was acknowledged by the Father in raising Christ to new life.

How does this affect me? I put myself under Christ's protection by the expression of total faith and trust in him which is Baptism, turning away from all other supports, a total act of conversion to Christ. That is, I am baptised into his death, and so enter into his death, accepting his offering of his life as my own. Neither this nor its repetition at the Easter renewal can be lightly or carelessly done. I believe that Christ's death and burial become my own death and burial. In the same way I am raised to life with Christ, and I believe that Christ's risen life is also my own risen life.

Action:

Prepare for the renewal of baptismal vows by considering what a renewal of life in Christ should involve.

Easter Sunday

> *Then the other disciple who had reached the tomb*
> *first also went in; he saw and he believed. Till this*
> *moment they had failed to understand the teaching*
> *of scripture, that he must rise from the dead.* (Jn 20:8-9)
> *åβ*Readings: Ac 10:34, 37-43; Col 3:1-4 or 1 Co 5:6-8; Jn 20:1-9

✠

What is this new life in Christ, which is now my life? Paul writes that we are yet to be transformed. In 2 Corinthians 3:18 he writes that through the Spirit "we are to grow brighter and brighter as we are turned into the image that we reflect"; and in Philippians 3:21, "he will *transfigure* these wretched bodies of ours into copies of his glorious body." These are still in the future tense. Here, however, in Colossians, the writer suggests that we have already been transformed and are waiting only to be *revealed* in all our glory, when Christ is revealed. What will the risen body and the risen life be like?

Some progress can be made through 1 Corinthians 15. First Paul says this is a stupid question (v. 35), but then he goes on to explain a little, in these steps:

1. There will be continuity with the present: "each sort of seed gets its own body" (v. 38).

2. There will be change: "not all flesh is the same flesh" (v. 39).

3. What is sown is perishable/contemptible/weak, but what is raised is imperishable/glorious/powerful (vv. 42-43).

4. The life principle will no longer be the human soul but the Spirit (v. 44).

These tell us little, but do tell us something. Each of the changes is a transfer into the sphere of the divine, of the God who is imperishable, glorious and powerful, and a Spirit. It is also clear in 1 Corinthians 15 that the Resurrection of Christ is the model and pattern of our own resurrection, so our body will presumably have the same properties as Christ was seen to have in the meetings after the Resurrection.

There is, of course, no story of the Resurrection itself. Only Matthew tells us that there was a great earthquake, and an angel of the Lord came to roll away the great stone. The primary evidence of the Resurrection was not the empty tomb, but the meetings with the Risen Lord, given in the traditional form by Paul (*1 Co* 15:3-5). In today's Gospel reading Peter sees the cloths, and the separation of the cloths seems to be somehow evidence that Jesus has risen, which convinces the Beloved Disciple. Perhaps the positioning of the cloths shows that somehow the risen body passed through them without disturbing them. Perhaps

Peter is held in check because he has not yet annulled his triple denial of his Master by the triple confession of his love, which is to follow in John 21:15-17.

After the end of the Gospel reading the story of Mary Magdalen continues with the touching account of her encounter with the Risen Lord, whom she had mistaken for the gardener. A feature of all the meetings recorded in the Gospels is that Jesus was somehow changed, in a way which made it difficult for his friends and disciples to recognise him. But here again it is love that is important and that enables both Mary and the Beloved Disciple to recognise the Risen Lord. It is the same for all his disciples.

Action:

Bring Easter joy to at least three people!